A Box in the Basement

To Diane,
Please enjoy these
stories of my interesting
family and friends.
my friend.
Eric Hodgkins

by Eric Hodgkins

Dedication

*To my grandmother, Matilda Loepp, whose lifetime of saving photographs, letters,
and other mementos of her loved ones has led to their proper recognition in this book.*

First Printing

Eric Hodgkins, Author

Published by
Dementi Milestone Publishing
www.dementimilestonepublishing.com

ISBN: 978-1-7330268-1-9

Graphic design by Amy Mendelson Design

To obtain a copy of this book contact Dementi Milestone Publishing
www.dementibooks.com

Introduction

Me walking my mother's dog, Rambo, less than a week after my heart attack.

I was worried that this book wouldn't get finished. At the end of September, 2018, it almost didn't. I called 911 as I had a feeling like an elephant was sitting on my chest. After four short, but interminably long minutes, the ambulance showed up. The EMTs asked who had the problem with shouts. I pointed to my chest as I walked to them. I couldn't speak. They had me walk up the steps of the ambulance, but I fell against the side wall. They caught me and put me in the gurney. I saw my morning commute in fast motion and backwards, as the ambulance was screaming east on Route 50, a road I had driven on for decades. In the preparation room of Fairfax Hospital, I was told I was having a heart attack. In the next room, the life-saving stent was put in me while I was awake, watching like it was on TV. It was in the ICU where it hit me that this book almost wasn't made, and it upset me.

In the fall of 2017, after finding a stash of photographs, letters and other items that belonged to my grandmother, I was able to run these things by my mother, Virginia Hodgkins and her sister, Reesy Hasson. In their 80s, they were able to tell me various stories and anecdotes and details; contextualizing some of the photos and other items I found. I had posted some of these stories on Facebook and was pleasantly surprised by the tremendous response to them. Without my mom and my aunt, many of these stories, general ideas and details would have been lost forever. They enjoyed being interviewed about their father, mother, two brothers and other important people from the past; many of whom I had never met. With this new information, I was able to understand my mother and her sister a little more; the void left by the passing of some of the great and important people of their lives.

When my grandmother stayed with us for the first two years of the 80's decade, we thought and worried about her age and her health, but we didn't think to ask her about her personal and family stories from decades past. As a teenager, not well-versed in her background, I didn't even know the right questions to ask had I asked them. She did say to me that she was excited that she was alive during a visit by Halley's Comet in 1910 and was looking forward to its next close pass by earth in 1986. Just from a short conversation, I would learn things from her. Unfortunately, she did not make that date.

I encourage you to find family heirlooms, photographs, letters, and any other items that connect you to earlier generations. Talk to those older family members who can give the stories behind the items you find; who can tell you who the people are in the old photos and what the occasion was. Without context from a parent or grandparent, an old water pitcher is just an old water pitcher. With context, that simple object may represent an epic immigration journey, privation during the Great Depression, or sacrifice during war time. Seniors, whether they are grandparents, parents, aunts or uncles, get eased out to the peripheries of family conversations and events because they have difficulty participating with disabilities and age. Keep these loved ones included. They deserve it. When interviewed about personal and family stories connected to items and photos, they can feel that sense of joy and pride from those landmark events in their lives; and celebrate important figures they lost so many decades ago. While you are making them feel happy by simply including them in conversation, they are doing so much more for you and your ongoing family by giving you information that would have otherwise been lost forever. Before that interview, make sure you find the family heirlooms, whatever form they take, perhaps in the living room, perhaps in the bedrooms, perhaps in the garage, perhaps in the attic, or just perhaps in a box in the basement.

"I'm young; I'm handsome; I'm fast. I can't possibly be beat."

— Muhammad Ali

The Time My Four-Year-Old Sister Told Muhammad Ali He Wasn't the Greatest

This is Ali as heavyweight champ in 1979 because he beat Leon Spinks in a rematch. I was 12 and my sister was 4. In LAX she sat on his lap, he and his bodyguards asked, "Who is the greatest?" She said, "Gerd Muller" as we are a soccer family. Ali and his guys were speechless. My mom and I said, "Oh my God Gina, no. Muhammad Ali is the greatest." They still had their index fingers up indicating who is number one. I think we tried to get Gina to put her index finger up.

We went on the airplane and lo and behold Ali did too. He was at the end of first class and I was at the beginning of econo across from him. So, I stared at him in awe. After a long period of time, he looked at me and winked and smiled. That did the trick. He dealt with this a million times.

A pretty lady came from the back of the plane and flirted, yapped and giggled; and then gave him her phone number.

This picture is in the tram at Dulles taking us from the plane to the airport. Ali waved my sister over to be on his lap again. My mom lifted the camera, then the flirty lady forced herself between Ali and his bodyguard and smiled like they were together all along. This left me out of the picture.

Walking out of the tram, into the airport, I held Ali's hand. He was unbelievably charismatic and everybody was drawn to him. I think he was the most recognizable, famous person on earth. He loved engaging people. I think he was at peace after all the past controversies. He loved people, especially children. And, I would like my sister to know that Muhammad Ali was the Greatest.

2

"Friendships are born on the field of athletic strife and the real gold of competition. Awards become corroded, friends gather no dust."

— Jesse Owens

Bill Devers: Greatness, Humility, and Humor at Age 15 Frozen in Time

1984 sports awards ceremony, my junior year. I am wearing the blue short sleeve shirt at the boys soccer table. I am next to a red headed senior wearing a blue jacket. We had hung out all the time freshman summer, sophomore year and summer. He was the one who pushed me to run cross country in 10th grade with him. He introduced me to the coach and the team. I would not have done it on my own. This is Bill Devers, and we were best friends. We both did cross country, track, and soccer. He was a year ahead of me. He was a tremendous athlete. At one point he was the fastest cross country runner along with other distances. He did hurdles. As a soccer player he was a fullback who covered the field fast. Players could not get past him. One example: I ran an 880 (half mile) heat in 2:08. I thought that was very good. Bill ran the next heat in 1:54; a stunning time. He certainly could have competed in college. Alas, his knee would give out some times. By his senior year, he drifted away some due to injury and a girlfriend. Even so, we are still sitting next to each other in this picture.

As he was a bit older than me and could do feats most people could not, he was heroic. I looked up to him. Despite all that talent he was unpretentious, friendly, fun, and funny; a good person. People were drawn to him, guys and girls.

Several years ago someone told me that Bill passed away. This person had no other information, so I held on to the idea that this was a mistaken, confused rumor. Well, I confirmed last night that Bill passed away in 2004 at the age of 38. The last time I saw him, my mom and I were at his wedding so long ago. He had joined the Navy and moved around. I had returned home from teaching English in Asia in 2003 for seven out of the eight previous years. We had gone our own ways and lost contact. Even so, it makes me sick I didn't search and find him.

I went to my first concert with him: the Kinks at the Capital Center. I remember Ray Davies said, "Hello Landover!" Funny. We collected comic books, played tennis, and played soccer in the yard; and went to movies. One example of his great sense of humor: in his house at the top of Country Hill, he had two orange cats exactly the same except one was horribly overweight. So I visited and saw the fat cat. Next time I see the normal-sized cat. I say, "What happened? Wasn't he bigger?" Bill says, "He went on a diet." Next time I visit, I see the fat cat again and Bill says, "He went back to his old ways." It was quite a while before I saw the two cats together like they were in on the joke. I mourn the bright, cheerful, charismatic guy I knew so well so long ago.

3

"I will go anywhere and do anything in order to communicate the love of Jesus to those who do not know Him or have forgotten Him."

— Mother Cabrini

Dr. Daniel V. Moore, a Man of Action during Landmark Disasters of History

One hundred and one years, 3 months and 18 days ago at 1:40 PM, Dr. Daniel V. Moore got up from lunch and heard a sound like a muffled bass drum. It was May 7, 1915 and Dr. Moore, my mother's Godfather, heard the torpedo from a German U-boat hit the Lusitania. He was going to Liverpool to volunteer his services as a surgeon to the British War Office. Instead, he ended up in Life Boat #14. Before taking a 12-foot jump, he got a ship singer in a boat. He then pulled a ship barber loose and in. As #14 filled with water, they tried to bail out with the women's hats. He swam to a keg after #14 went down and hung on for some hours. As one of the 764 survivors, he was picked up by a rescue ship, Brock. He put a splint on a 10-year-old boy's fractured leg. That boy, Frank Hook, then asked to see the funny papers.

From a Dublin hospital he gave a deposition and his famous telegram was sent describing how the Lusitania zigzagged for a while before being hit; and how they had seen a black, oblong object about two miles off with glasses. The passengers had talked at lunch about the submarine and how they thought it was a friendly.

The U.S. Mixed Claims Commission ruled against Germany and awarded Dr. Moore $10,000 in 1923. He suffered physical problems and was not able to work for 18 months.

The man who would become my mother's Godfather in 1932, was still recovering from health issues related to the Lusitania sinking where 1,198 souls were lost. His convalescence would go late into 1916. Dr. Moore would try to save lives in two more landmark events in history. One was 10 years earlier: as a young man he went to Northern California to offer medical help in the aftermath of the Great 1906 San Francisco Earthquake. Fires lasted for days and the fire chief was killed. Eighty percent of the city was destroyed and buildings were unstable. The quake was felt from Oregon to LA. It is not known how many of the 3,000 dead he tried to save or how many of the 300,000 newly homeless he treated, but the good doctor was a good Catholic who took very seriously good works.

Dr. Moore continued his medical education and work in New York City at Columbus Hospital, one of 67 institutions (including orphanages and schools for the poor) in the United States founded by Mother Cabrini. Out of the Kingdom of Lombardy-Venetia, Austrian Empire, Mother Cabrini in 1877 asked Pope Leo XIII for permission to set up missions in China. He said, "Not to the East, but to the West." He sent

Dr. Daniel V. Moore Dies In Sioux City; Rites Here Wed.

SIOUX CITY, (Special)—Dr. Daniel V. Moore, former prominent Sioux City physician, who had had no fewer than seven close brushes with death—the last as a passenger aboard the steamer Lusitania—is dead at the age of 73.

Dr. Moore, one of 734 survivors of the 3,700 who boarded the disaster-marked ship May 1, 1915.

her to help the millions of poor Italian immigrants who were flooding into that emerging power to the West, the United States of America.

In the afternoon of March 25, 1911 at 4:45, fire engines and ambulances screamed toward the Asch Building on Greene St and Washington Place. Dr. Daniel V. Moore was in one of those ambulances. A new type of horror was about to welcome the doctor, for this was the Triangle Shirtwaist Factory fire, the deadliest industrial disaster in the history of the city. One hundred and forty-six people died, mostly newly arrived Jewish and Italian immigrant women, 16 to 23 years of age. The owners locked the doors to the stairwells and exits to prevent breaks and theft. It was hard for rescuers to get in because of the falling bodies. Women fainted in the streets, men rushed the police cordon. A man and a woman kissed before jumping from the 9th floor.

There was nothing to do for the 62 who jumped, but the doctor surely treated some of the 71 injured. This disaster led to legislation for factory safety standards and spurred the growth of the International Ladies' Garment Workers' Union.

Dr. Moore brought a prized possession with him on the Lusitania, a diploma signed by Mother Cabrini from Columbus Hospital (later Cabrini Medical Center). It went down with the ship. Such was her importance to him that this was a loss to him. She was important to Catholics and many others. Close to 30 years after her death, Pope Pius XII canonized her on July 7, 1946. Mother Cabrini became a Saint.

Dr. Moore moved to Sioux City, Iowa in 1920 and lived there until 1948. He outlived his six brothers. His sister kept house for him, as he did not marry. She passed away in 1939. He had a practice in Sioux City and nearby Yankton, South Dakota where his brother had been mayor.

My aunt told me that he had a romantic interest, but alas information came out that insanity ran in her family. He shied away. My mother does not know how her parents knew the doctor. It could have been through Church as her mother was Catholic. I asked her why, in her opinion, he was chosen to be her Godfather. She said, with certainty, that it was because he was a good Catholic. My mom met Dr. Moore when she was 3 years old. He gave her a two-foot tall cloth doll that she promptly named "Nelly."

In 1948, Dr. Moore was getting confused. He would drive to California in a very old Ford for no apparent reason. The police picked him up for driving erratically and committed him to a hospital in Cherokee,

Iowa. He may have forgotten who he was. He didn't know people's names. He asked for his old friend, my grandfather, David Loepp. But, he didn't know his name, so he asked for the former mayor with the term "Your Honor." Please send me Your Honor. Someone figured out that meant former mayor, David Loepp.

My grandfather then acted as his lawyer and guardian until Loepp died in 1950. Then my grandmother took over as guardian for Dr. Moore until he died in 1953.

Perhaps the horror of the disasters he witnessed and endured finally broke him. To this day my mother and aunt send cards indicating that a mass and prayers will be said for the recipient. Mr. Loepp was a Lutheran who attended a Methodist Church, perhaps for the music. It was Mrs. Loepp who was the Catholic, also of German background. Two of her sisters became Sisters (pictured on page 4). She considered becoming a nun herself. My brothers and I wondered why it was so important to our mom that we go to Saint Leo's Catholic Church in Fairfax City. At age 50, I can now see that for people like my mom, my aunt, their mother; and certainly for Mother Cabrini and Dr. Moore, their faith is no joke. The doctor lived it. I will say a prayer for Dr. Daniel V. Moore.

My mother, Virginia Loepp, at 3 years old, circa 1935, holding the doll that her Godfather, Dr. Daniel V. Moore, gave her.

4

*"For in every adult there dwells the child that was,
and in every child there lies the adult that will be."*

— John Connolly, The Book of Lost Things

A Conversation with a Man at My Nephew's Birthday Party

I went to my little nephew's birthday at the Ashland, VA Museum. It was train-themed. He got to run the electric train and tour the historic caboose.

I talked to a nice, older man there who has fond memories of Ashland. In the 1950s and 1960s, a Christmas train used to bring three and four-year-old kids and their parents from Richmond to Ashland. At the end of the 20-minute ride, to their astonishment, Santa Claus would greet them at the station. He would magically know the names of the children (with the help of his Helper). This man was still excited about that train ride from Richmond to Ashland when I talked to him last Thursday night.

5

"When a great man dies, for years the light he leaves behind him, lies on the paths of men."

— Henry Wadsworth Longfellow

The Marine in WWI Joined the Army in WWII

This is my mother's father, David Loepp, at Marine Corps boot camp in Parris Island, South Carolina in 1918 on the opposite page. To the right, Major David Loepp is with four other officers, most likely of the Allied Military Government, in Rome, 1944. My mother is holding his military satchel in the two pictures below from his Army uniform in the Second World War.

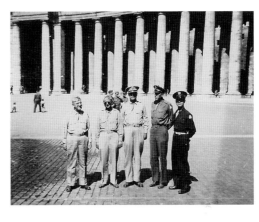

As a German American, he spoke German fluently. With a Law Degree from the University of Chicago

and being Mayor of Sioux City, Iowa he was assigned to be Military Governor of an Italian city as the Allies rolled up Italy. With his qualifications, he was to be part of the prosecution team at Nuremberg to try the Nazis. But, his chest started to hurt again. He had complained of chest pains over the years. The doctors would tell him he had nerves or stress and to take a break. They never successfully diagnosed his heart disease. He died of a massive heart attack in 1950, leaving behind a wife, two sons and two daughters (one being my mom, the other being my Aunt Reesy who became a lawyer in her own right).

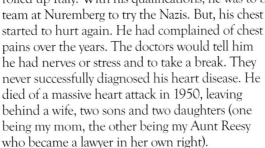

My mom always thought that her dad going through boot camp as a middle-aged man was too much for him and sped up the end. He had run for U.S. Congress. Who knows if he would have run again or run for something else.

The loss of this man 66 years ago still affects our family to this day. My mother believes that this hit her younger brother, Robby, very hard. He was the youngest child at only 15. He took a very difficult path in life after that. All four children attained higher education and became successful. With that, I believe they have lived with a sadness in the background their whole adult lives. The older brother, Dave, was a geologist who had worked in South America and in the oil fields of Texas who may have also passed from a heart attack. He died too early in 1981. He should not have gone before his mother (my grandmother) did. As she lived with us at the time, I heard her reaction to the news that my mother brought her about her brother Dave, named after her father, the great patriarch and veteran who also died too early. I heard a terrible wailing I had never heard before. She (my grandmother) died not long after in 1982. I believe that my grandfather, David Loepp's death in 1950 reverberated through the decades to this day. My three brothers and one sister never met him, but miss him. My mom can talk about her dad like it was yesterday. I can see in her eyes she misses him.

My grandfather, David F. Loepp, conducting a swearing-in as judge in occupied Italy in 1944, as the Allies were pushing the German army back up mainland Italy.

My grandfather, David F. Loepp, presiding as judge in occupied Italy in 1944, as the Allies were pushing the German army back up mainland Italy. After many months in North Africa and then many more in Italy, Major Loepp, on behalf of the Allied Military Government, became Military Governor in Viterbo, a city north of Rome, after the Allies moved the German army out of that area.

14

6

"One of the good things about the way the Gulf War ended in 1991 is, you'd see the Vietnam veterans marching with the Gulf War veterans."

— George H. W. Bush

Memorial Day, 1992

I believe this is 1992, Memorial Day weekend in the parking lot of Tara's favorite restaurant up here, El Torito in Arlington, Virginia. It doesn't exist here anymore. Years later I ate at one in Japan. They had a great brunch on the weekends. They would serve Mimosas and Bloody Marys. I was afraid she wouldn't like anything up here because her city, New Orleans, has some of the greatest food in the world.

We are posing in front of motorcycles that belong to veterans, mostly of the Vietnam War. You can see the American flags and the black POW flag. Their part of the parade is called "Rolling Thunder." On the Sunday before Memorial Day, thousands of these veterans sit quietly on their bikes in the Pentagon parking lot, and then, at noon they start their motorcycles at the same time, sounding like thunder. They go across the Memorial Bridge from the Arlington Cemetery toward the Lincoln Memorial and end up at the Vietnam Wall. While going across the Memorial Bridge and slowly traversing that route, they sound like rolling thunder; and it recalls Operation Rolling Thunder in 1964, a largescale escalation of American involvement in Vietnam. It had only been five years since they started this idea to bring attention to POWs (prisoners of war) and MIAs (missing in action). But, I think there was one other reason for the thousands of Vietnam veterans coming to Washington D.C. on Memorial Day starting in the 1980s. They had not come to D.C., nor were they invited, for the whole decade of the 1970s. They were finally getting their parade and recognition that was never given to them when they returned home from the jungles of Southeast Asia.

7

"Walking with a friend in the dark is better than walking alone in the light."

— *Helen Keller*

Driving Half the Length of the United States for a Friend

I had met Tara in 1992 when my brother, Scott and a friend of mine went into a bar in Georgetown. We talked to Tara and some of her friends from a small women's college near American University. I found a bunch of flowers on the way to the bar and we passed them out as they were an icebreaker to meet our new friends. I had asked Tara if she was wearing a weave and she then gave me a solid right hook to the gut. Note to self: Don't ask a black girl if she's wearing a weave. She may have been unhappy with the flowers too once I came clean about that. But, it did lead to a friendship that lasts to this day.

The two photos are of us in front of my 1989 Mustang around 1992. I had driven that car down to New Orleans with friends in 1994 and I met Tara's family. After teaching English in Korea in 1995, I was doing temp jobs back here. That's when I heard Tara had gotten Leukemia. I dropped my job, jumped in my Mustang and drove 1,500 miles to New Orleans by myself this time. I slept in the car at a rest stop perhaps in Alabama. The Reeds truly didn't believe I was coming. They thought the words were a nice gesture. I knocked on the door and Mrs. Reed went up and told Tara, "It's Eric." Tara thought she meant I was on the phone. She was able to drive to go to the hospital, but otherwise took it slow; even spent much of her time in bed. I could see she wasn't well and was moving and speaking more slowly. I didn't know what I could do for my friend. Thank God her brother was a match and could then get the bone marrow transplant after my visit. When I had left the Crescent City, we didn't know if there was a match out there. Twenty years later we are still yapping on the phone all the time.

MERRY CHRISTMAS — HAPPY NEW YEAR

The Hodgkins

David Scott Terry

8

"When someone you love becomes a memory, the memory becomes a treasure."

— Unknown

Merry Christmas and Happy New Year, 1964

Merry Christmas and Happy New Year from the Hodgkins in, most likely, 1964-1965. I had used this photo in October on the occasion of two of my brothers' birthdays. This time I have pulled the camera back to show that this is actually a Christmas card sent from my father's mother's neighborhood in Massachusetts to my mother's mother in Iowa.

Brant Rock Beach, along Cape Cod between Boston and Plymouth Plantation, had pebbles and rocks on one side and a regular beach with sand on the other. Having experienced this rocky beach in many Novembers of my childhood, when we finally saw the famous rock south of there in Plymouth it wasn't a surprise for we had already seen those types of rocks large and small in and out of the water. There were food shacks around Brant Rock that would sell delicious fast food like fried clams and French fries, my mom's favorite.

My brothers and I did not know or remember that they had blonde hair as small children. I, on the other hand, was a towhead with very blonde hair almost to high school. Even then I went light in the summer. I believe this has very much to do with our grandmother on my father's side being 100 percent Swedish American. Even in old age, she remembered a few Swedish words her mother had taught her.

The other thing we did not know was that our grandmother in Iowa, Mrs. Loepp, had kept this simple Christmas card with her for the rest of her life from 1964 to 1982. As my parent's house was her final residence, there were some boxes with her belongings stored in the basement. Only this year did I find this box and discover the things she saved and valued.

9

""Life is a journey, not a destination."

— Often credited to Ralph Waldo Emerson

Station Wagon to Massachusetts, 1975

In the summer of 1975 my dad woke me and my three older brothers up and got us into the Mercury station wagon. We were taking a vacation to his mother's near Boston. At the start of the eight-hour trip from our home in Fairfax, VA, we would get a dozen donuts and chocolate milk at Mr Donut or one of the others. The optical illusion on the U.S. map had me feeling like New York City was close to Boston, but it was only the halfway point. The second half of the trip was brutal for kids. If we got out of line, dad would threaten to pull the car over. I think it's fair to say it was usually brother #3, Scott's fault.

Scott is in the stocks in this photo near the famous rock in Plymouth. I am clearly delighted by this off to the left with the blonde hair. As the youngest brother, four years Scott's junior, I would always be on the losing side verbally, physically and with teasing and torture. So, even though this was pretend, I still enjoyed it. Brother #2, Dave, is in the yellow shirt.

Our cousin, Bobby, is in the white top. He and his brother, Gary, would come out of Revere, Massachusetts to join us. Bobby knew sign language because both of their parents were deaf. Their mother, Patty, was my father's sister. My father, his two brothers and their parents never did learn sign language because their mother, the tough Swedish American, said she won't be able to survive in this world without reading lips. So, we would converse with Aunt Patty and Uncle Bill. We just had to remember to face them and enunciate. Bill was great. He would actually tell us jokes and stories. My brothers and I felt that our mother would over-enunciate and speak too loudly with Bill and Patty as she got into the spirit of talking to them. We were probably wrong as she successfully communicated with them, and I was hit and miss.

My mother would fly in with our baby sister from Iowa to join us. She came from her 25-year high school reunion. It seems that little Gina flew on a plane before any of her older brothers did.

10

"Every child is born a genius."

— *Albert Einstein*

The Language My Cousin Bob Used as a Baby

My aunt Patty with her two boys, Bobby and Gary, in the early 1960s. Our cousin, Bob, the older of the two, is about the age of my brother, Dave. Bob's first language was not English. It wasn't even a spoken language. It was sign language, as both of his parents, Patty and Bill, were deaf. My mother recalls seeing the baby, Bobby, only months old communicating with his parents using sign language. He would sign that he wanted milk or water and addressed his parents as "Mom" and "Dad" using their preferred language.

11

*"What you leave behind is not what is engraved in stone monuments,
but what is woven into the lives of others."*

— Pericles

A Great Grandmother Half the Age of the United States

How is it that I am 1/8 Irish? The answer to that question: the lady in pink. We had gone on the long trips by car to Boston and Brant Rock many years in a row, but we would often go around Thanksgiving, as my father's birthday was around that time. But, this trip in July of 1975 was a different and special occasion: our great grandmother (my father's father's mother) was turning 100 years old. Margaret was the 10th child of a couple who was from Ireland, and she was the only one of that family born in America. She had married a man in Boston who was born in England named Walter Hodgkins. That is how I get my English last name and how I am 1/8 English.

Dave is #57, Terry is the tallest, I am next and Scott is on the right. My dad is holding new little sister Gina. My mother is taking this picture. My father's mother (my grandmother) Muriel is sitting to the right. Muriel (Olssen) Hodgkins is the reason I am 1/4 Swedish and most likely the reason for my blonde hair. Our great grandmother, Margaret or Maggie, was more than 99 years older than Gina in this picture. I have dirt and grass on the back of my clothes because Scott told Cousin Gary who was older and bigger than me, to wrestle me before we got into this house. I think I flopped like a dead fish and had to say "uncle." Like Detective Clouseau keeping an eye out for a surprise attack from Cato, I keep an eye on Scott and Gary. I believe Gary beat Scott in arm wrestling.

My dad's mother, Muriel, is smiling in this photo; this was a rare thing to see. She loved her mother-in-law, Margaret. In the 1930s and 1940s, Margaret used to bake birthday cakes for Muriel's children: my dad, Patty, Dick and Ronnie. Margaret would bake the cake and then take a city bus to deliver it to Muriel's house in Boston.

Soon after this photo was taken, Margaret told my mom in a matter of fact fashion that she did not want to see her next birthday. And, she didn't. She missed it by a month or two in the Bicentennial year of our country that she had witnessed the second half of. Even though she had five living children in the area who cared about her and one, Louise, who cared for her, Margaret lost her husband in the 1950s and a son (my father's father) in 1961. Louise, her caretaker/daughter, had lost her first husband, a soldier in WWI, to a gas attack by the Germans. Margaret, who was also known as Maggie, had been through a lot and was ready to go. I had a little conversation with sweet Margaret, and for the life of me, I can't remember what was said.

12

Born Edwin Eugene "Buzz" Aldrin, Jr. on January 20, 1930, in Montclair, New Jersey. The nickname "Buzz" originated in childhood: his little sister mispronounced the word "brother" as "buzzer." His family shortened the nickname to "Buzz." Aldrin would make it his legal first name in 1988.

— History.com

How my Aunt Got Her Name

Happy Birthday to my aunt Reesy today. This is her as a child with her (and my mom's) older brother, David. My whole life my aunt has been known as Reesy. I didn't even know her actual full name, Marie Therese Loepp. She got her nickname, which she would use the rest of her life, about 88 years ago when the very young David couldn't pronounce "Therese." He would say, "Reesa Reesa" when referring to his new infant sister.

Pardon my interjection here, but I would like to make my own guesstimate; and that is that she never considered being called anything other than her nickname because she so admired and loved her brother who would become a great geologist. I know that she reveres family members, and she wouldn't have it any other way.

Like her father and brother, Reesy would earn honors and continue with higher education after the University of Iowa. She taught in Iowa, Nebraska, and Washington D.C. She worked in Wyoming at one point for a petroleum company, perhaps related to her brother's job. After getting her law degree at George Washington University Law School, she was admitted to the Bar in the District of Columbia in 1964. She worked at the Interstate Commerce Commission where I believe she met her husband-to-be, a judge. Later she and her husband would practice before the U.S. Court of Veterans Appeals, representing disabled veterans on benefits cases. Anyway, Happy Birthday to (Reesa Reesa) Reesy.

13

"Your name is not Eve Harrington. It is Gertrude Slescynski..."

— Addison DeWitt in All About Eve

The Curly Haired Guy from Milwaukee

In the winter of 1974, my mother was at home on Hunter Street reading the local newspaper of this city, *The Fairfax Journal*. Back then, newspapers would have an article about a movie that was coming into town. The movie that was coming into town was *Young Frankenstein*, starring Gene Wilder. My brother, Dave, would see that movie at Loehmann's Plaza in Falls Church as a junior high schooler. It was his favorite movie and he quoted it so often, I knew the jokes by heart before even seeing it myself.

Anyway, the article was about Gene Wilder. My mom was surprised to see that this world-famous movie star went to Iowa University like she did and that he was a year younger than her. Then it hit her: she knew this person. She remembered a man with wavy, curly blonde hair and big blue eyes with long eyelashes. She said he had an expressive face and you expected him to be funny. She remembered he had a somewhat high voice. He acted in the theater at Iowa University. My mom saw a play with him in it either in 1953 or 1954. We see him below putting on makeup and acting in *Harvey* and other plays in 1953. And, you can see his senior picture in 1955 and my mom's in 1954. Seeing this co-student in a play was interesting to her because he was dating one of her girlfriends, a beautiful, slightly overweight blonde. She often saw them walking down the halls and around the campus together. She said, "That's Jerry!" She knew him as Jerry Silberman from Milwaukee, Wisconsin. His given name was Jerome, but people called him Jerry. Only years later did he adopt his professional name, Gene Wilder.

14

"Bless the seven little men who have been so kind to me, and—and may my dreams come true. Amen. Oh yes, and please make Grumpy like me."

— Snow White in Snow White and the Seven Dwarfs

Grump Pa and Aunt Patty

When my father and his siblings, Patty, Dick and Ronnie, were children in the 1930s and 1940s, they noticed that their grandfather, Walter Hodgkins, would frown and often wasn't in a good mood. So much so, that my father, his two brothers, and their mother, Muriel, may have called him "Grump Pa." Perhaps he wasn't happily entering old age. Patty was the exception here. She liked him and worried about him continually saying, "What about Grandpa?"

One may believe she liked him because she was the only girl or because she was deaf, not noticing his mood or perceiving what others thought of him. But, she told my mother that she tried to make him smile; she was aware of his demeanor. Whenever my brothers and I met Patty, it would lift our spirits because with passion and enthusiasm she would tell us she loved us and how wonderful we were. You would walk away from that feeling great.

Well, Patty finally melted his heart and won him over. Even in her teenage and adult years Patty had a close relationship with Grandma (Maggie) and Grandpa (Walter) Hodgkins. In the late 1940s and early 1950s, the two grandparents would have Patty over once a week for dinner. They were excited about seeing Patty and looked forward to it. Grandma would cook a special meal and Grandpa would shave and wear his best suit jacket and tie. Patty would get dolled up and wear pretty dresses and ribbons. I believe this ritual continued until Walter, who went from "Grump Pa" to the man anticipating every weekly dinner date with his charming, darling granddaughter, passed away in the 1950s.

15

¹⁹ And it became known to all the inhabitants of Jerusalem, so that the field was called in their own language Akeldama, that is, Field of Blood.) ²⁰ "For it is written in the Book of Psalms, "'May his camp become desolate, and let there be no one to dwell in it';….

— Acts 1:16-25 English Standard Version (ESV)

The Median Strip at Route 301

My 1995 BMW, Little Red, was able to take me to a spot in Port Royal, VA about 100 miles from my house: what 152 years ago was Garrett's farm, the place where President Lincoln's assassin, John Wilkes Booth, was shot, became paralyzed, and died some hours later. This is a few miles from the Rappahannock River.

The problem is the farm with its house and barn don't exist anymore. There isn't anything marking the exact spots of the tobacco barn where he was shot or the porch where he died. Going south on Route 301, a historical marker says you are two miles away, but you are not allowed to stop there. You know you have reached the spot when there is a swath of signs saying, "no parking, stopping or standing, tow-away zone." They obviously had problems with history buffs and gawkers in the past. So I continued my gawking by doing a U-turn a couple of miles past. Coming up Route 301 north, we see the "Assassin's End" sign very close to the spot. Then you drive up a hundred yards or so and see a matching swath of "no parking, stopping or standing, tow-away zone" signs for the northerly direction. Of the hundreds of miles I've driven on the 301, the 3, the 17 and others, that's the only place I see those signs.

Here's the safety issue: this historical spot (even if it is only woods, dirt and trash) is literally in the median strip between the northbound and southbound lanes of a highway where cars are going 55 to 80 mph. How many history buffs have been run over trying to get to a wooded median strip where they will find nothing? FYI, I did not try to run across the 301 in search of ghosts.

  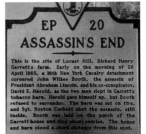 

"Until one has loved an animal a part of one's soul remains unawakened."

— Anatole France

My Mom's Childhood Pet

Happy Birthday to my mom on April 4. In the 1930's in the Loepp's neighborhood in Sioux City, Iowa, sometimes a man would walk down the street with a pony and a camera. My Aunt Reesy thinks it was 25 cents for a picture. This photograph on the opposite page is the result. This may be 1935 or 1936 with my mom on front and her older sister, Reesy, behind her.

A couple of years after this photo, a man who owned the lumberyard suggested to their father, the new mayor, that he lend him his pony for the kids. So, my mom and her family had a pet pony named Tiny during the Great Depression. They lived in a suburban neighborhood with streets, sidewalks, a driveway and a garage. They kept Tiny in the garage at night with a bale of hay. During the day their older brother, David, probably walked the pony around the yard and then tied him to the side of the house. One night a thunderstorm scared Tiny and she escaped the garage, jumped into the creek in their backyard and swam away. David was very upset when he found this out in the morning. He went all around the neighborhood and found Tiny about two miles away. Eleven-year-old David triumphantly walked the pony back home.

That fall my mom went back to school for first grade this time. The teacher asked the class if they had pets. The kids said they had cats, dogs, turtles and such. When my mom was called on, she said she had a pet pony. There was a gasp and the teacher said, "A pony?!"

Their father returned Tiny to Mr. Shoeneman, the lumberyard owner.

The other picture is of my mom with her current pet, a small dog named Rambo during her birthday in 2017.

17

> *"It will give our people at home the assurance that they are standing four-square behind our soldiers and sailors. And it will give our enemies demoralizing assurance that we mean business -that we, 130,000,000 Americans, are on the march to Rome, Berlin, and Tokyo."*

> — *State of the Union Message to Congress by President Franklin D. Roosevelt, January 11, 1944*

Easter Sunday, 1944

Easter Sunday, 1944; Sioux City, Iowa: Happy Easter from my mom's family, the Loepps, in front of their fireplace/cookout in their backyard before going to church. Mrs. Loepp (my mom's mother) is in the back. The avid Catholic and wife of the three-term former mayor is now in this picture worried, like so many others, worried about her husband overseas in the war. The teenage girl in the Sunday hat is my Aunt Reesy, and the girl without a hat is my mother. Mrs. Loepp paid a friend, who was a seamstress, to make both daughters' Easter suits (coat and skirt). Mom's was of a light wool. The man in the hat is my mom's Uncle Art (my mom's father's brother). In addition to Art's brother being in the war, all three of his sons were serving: one in the Pacific and two in the European theater. Two months after this photo one son would land in Normandy on D-Day, and eight months after this photo his other son would be fighting in the Battle of the Bulge. With this, 52-year-old Art said maybe he should join the Army. His wife, Mildred, was having none of it. She sarcastically said sure and maybe she'll join the WACS (Women's Army Corps).

Notice that my mother's little brother, Robby, is wearing a Fez cap (originated in the Ottoman Empire). How is a boy in Iowa in 1944 wearing a Fez? My grandfather, David F. Loepp, was shipped out to Algiers, Algeria in November, 1943. He sent a Fez back to his youngest son from North Africa as a souvenir. More than two months after this photo, he would be Military Governor of Viterbo, a central Italian city north of Rome. As the Germans were shelling the city, Major David Loepp would get electricity, water and sewage restored. High priority was burying all the dead bodies.

Notice that my mother's oldest brother, the 17-year-old David Q. Loepp, is quite proudly wearing a white scarf. As a member of the Civil Air Patrol (CAP), he was given the dashing pilot scarf. You can see that he wrapped and tied it like the WWII pilots did. They were a civilian group who were ready for emergencies and such. David Q most likely met bomber pilots at the Sioux City Army Air Base (ordered built by then Mayor David F. Loepp and Congressman Harrington). Today that airport is called Sioux Gateway Airport/or Colonel Bud Day Field. At the time of this photo, the airbase was used to train B-17 Flying

Fortress and B-24 Liberator pilots. Every week my mom would hear the various bombers practicing low overhead. One day while washing her hair the Flying Fortresses flew so low and so loud she ran out of the house terrified that they were crashing. She looked up to make sure they would make it over the treetops, they seemingly barely did.

The reality of the war was all around. Their neighbors, the Pratts, eight houses up on Manor Circle, had an only child at 23 years of age. He flew The Hump, the India-China Airlift, over the Himalayan Mountains as a result of the Japanese blocking the Burma Road. They supplied U.S. forces in China and Chiang Kai-shek's Chinese forces. That flight was so dangerous that many of those planes went down never to be found. When this photo was taken, the Pratts' only boy was already missing with his plane somewhere in the Himalayas.

My mom recalls that the sermons at the Blessed Sacrament Catholic Church in Sioux City were about praying for peace, praying for the GI's; praying for everyone's loved ones to come home.

18

"April 13, 14, Friday, the Ides.
…. I struck boldly, and not as the papers say. I walked with a firm step through a
thousand of his friends, was stopped, but pushed on. A colonel was at his side.
I shouted Sic semper before I fired. In jumping broke my leg. I passed all his pickets, rode
sixty miles that night with the bone of my leg tearing the flesh at every jump.
I can never repent it, though we hated to kill…."

— Diary of John Wilkes Booth

Standing in the Way of John Wilkes Booth

Only recently did my friend, John, tell me that the old 9:30 Club was right near Ford's Theater, where John Wilkes Booth assassinated President Lincoln. In 1986/1987, when we got our pictures with the famous punk star, Wendy O Williams, because John interviewed her for GMU Radio, the shows started at 9:30 and the address was 930 F Street. I am pictured with Wendy O Williams on the opposite page. F St. crosses 10th St. Ford's Theater is on 10th between E and F streets. I did not know this 30 years ago. I was just concerned about the extraordinarily loud concert I was about to hear. I considered putting cotton in my ears but I didn't want to look like a nerd in that audience and be judged by people with Mohawks, purple hair, piercings and leather jackets with spikes. I go in there and most of those people were wearing earplugs. I was the odd one without ear protection. I'm sure I had reduced hearing for about half a day and then it came back.

The alley that goes in a line from the back of Ford's Theater, was called Baptist Alley in 1865, and it pointed towards 9th St. The alley that John, Wendy O Williams and I were standing in is perpendicular to Baptist Alley and leads out to F St. I just learned this through some research. What does this mean? It means that 121 or 122 years before I had my arm around that famous lady of punk, on Good Friday, April 14, 1865 at about 10:15 PM, John Wilkes Booth upon committing the most infamous crime in American history, had galloped away at full speed in a getaway trampling over the very spot where John and I posed with Wendy O. He took the horse from the back of the theater, rode up Baptist Alley and took a left onto our alley in the two pictures and exited out onto F Street.

In 1865 there was a black woman named Mary Jane Anderson who lived in an alley house in Baptist Alley with a view of the back of the theater. She saw Booth eight hours earlier behind the theater talking to a young lady, probably one of his many girlfriends. Ms. Anderson stared at him as he was the most famous actor in the country at that time and quite handsome. Then, around 9:00 PM she sees Booth walk a restless horse down her alley to the back of the theater. He then calls through the back door for someone to hold his horse. Finally, someone comes out and walks the horse back and forth as it won't stay still. Ms. Anderson hears the loud hoofs on the cobblestone. At about 10:15 PM Ms. Anderson sees Booth fly out of the back door of Ford's Theater, holding something that was glistening. That was the knife dripping with blood that Booth stabbed Major Rathbone in the arm with. Rathbone and his fiancee, Clara Harris, were guests of the Lincolns in the balcony box after General Ulysses Grant and his wife declined. Ms. Anderson saw Booth pull away from a theater goer trying to catch him, tear down Baptist Alley and take a left on the alley headed out to F and fly over the spot where countless New Wave, Punk, Metal, and other rock bands took breaks 120 years later.

I had no idea that that dark, dirty, smelly alley with oversized rats and plenty of dumpsters, where John and I posed with Wendy O Williams in, was witness to such a significant event in American history. After taking our pictures, John remembers seeing robed people with hoods, looking like monks, down the alley. Apparently, some actors at Ford's Theater were taking a break. A hundred and twenty years later and actors are still sneaking out the back door of Ford's Theater.

My friend, John Judge, with Wendy O Williams as part of his interview for George Mason University Radio in the alley behind the old 9:30 Club.

19

"In the previous administration, we Americanized the war in Vietnam. In this administration, we are Vietnamizing the search for peace."

— Richard Milhous Nixon, Address on the War in Vietnam, November 3, 1969

The Thing Andy Never Told Me

Happy Memorial Day. In the middle of this picture is Andy Smallwood. I played soccer with him for four years at Fairfax High School in the 1980s. He usually played fullback. The big guy on the right, another fullback, is Steve Myseros. In my childhood, I had lived in Fairview in Fairfax City. My street, Hunter Street, ended at a long street, Carolyn Avenue. When you go down the hill of that street, Steve's house would be on the right side. Adjacent to the backyard of the Myseros family was the backyard of the Smallwood family. Andy was one of eight children and was born a year after me in the 1960s.

According to my mom's best recollection, Mr. Smallwood was a Colonel in the Army in the late 1960s, serving in Vietnam. On September 8, 1969, a month and seven days after arriving in country, Lieutenant Colonel Eugene Smallwood, at an RVN (Republic of Vietnam) army base in Long An Province 25 miles southwest of Saigon, was a senior advisor to the South Vietnamese 50th Regiment, 25th Infantry Division with MACV (Military Assistance Command, Vietnam) Advisory Team 99. This was the announcement from U.S. Command:

Two U.S. military advisers were shot and killed Monday by a "mentally depressed" South Vietnamese soldier who then killed himself, the U.S. Command announced today.

The Americans were Lieutenant Colonel Eugene F. Smallwood, 42, of Fairfax, Virginia, and Major Anthony J. Broullon, 32, of Jackson Heights, New York.

He was in a safe zone in South Vietnam nowhere near any of the fighting. Tragically...inexplicably... at a military headquarters away from the action, a South Vietnamese Army guard went berserk and killed Mr. Smallwood and another man as they were exiting the compound, leaving behind a wife who was taking care of seven children and pregnant with the eighth. I believe Andy was the seventh, meaning he lost his father at a very young age. I believe the eighth child was a younger sister who would never know her father. Mrs. Smallwood, while she was pregnant with Andy's younger sister, was asked to come to Washington D.C. to ID her slain husband.

I was not aware of any of these things when I played soccer with Andy, a nice, affable person. I would just say: God bless the Smallwoods and especially Mrs. Smallwood who endured the harsh side of being a military spouse.

20

"That's the story of New Orleans — but that's also the story of America — a city that, for almost 300 years, has been the gateway to America's soul. Where the jazz makes you cry, the funerals make you dance — the bayou makes you believe all kinds of things…

— President Obama, September 28, 2015,

The Remarkable Mr. Reed and the Grand Dame
(the parents of my good friend of 25 years, Tara Reed)

The 4th of 12 children in a family out of the 9th Ward, Mr. Reed was a New Orleans Police Officer and then a DEA Officer in the 1970s; appointed to a commission to oversee the police in the 1980s. He established his own law firm. He was a Criminal District Court Judge of Orleans Parish when I met him in 1994. He recently ended his term as president of the NAACP, New Orleans Branch. He ran for District Attorney two or three times in the 80s and 90s against Harry Connick Sr, father of the famous jazz singer. He pushed each of those races to run-offs, but unfortunately lost.

A reminder of DAs in the Big Easy: James Garrison (1962-1973) spent valuable time, 1966-1969, chasing a JFK assassination conspiracy theory, not convicting one person. Kevin Costner played him in the 1991 film, *JFK*. In addition to capturing imaginary conspirators, apparently, the DA was taking $2,000 bribes from illegal pinball operations every two months for nine years… acquitted. But, the damage was done. Harry Connick Sr (1973-2003) became DA. Dubbed "The Singing District Attorney," he would sing in clubs in the French Quarter, especially Maxwell's Toulouse Cabaret. In 1989, one thing he didn't sing about was returning gambling records to an arrested gambler. The Singing District Attorney claimed that the poor gambler needed them for his tax returns… acquitted. Unlike the previous DA, he was able to keep his job.

I don't know what else the eminently qualified Judge Reed could have added to his remarkable resume to defeat Connick, other than singing some snappy tunes at Maxwell's. I would not be surprised if some shenanigans were employed against Mr. Reed in those elections. When Tara informed me of his background at the time, my reaction was: Why isn't he running for Mayor?

Mrs. Reed, out of Covington above Lake Pontchartrain, has done many things in her own right: English teacher, model, running restaurants, clothing stores and even a finishing school for etiquette... to name a few. There are pictures of her family members in the famous D-Day Museum in New Orleans. Some people believe that the only sin worse than being a bad person is being inauthentic or boring or forgettable. Mrs. Reed is innocent of that. If you meet her, you will never forget her. She is an original and, I believe, a product of the South and specifically New Orleans. Tourists will eat gumbo or jambalaya to try to capture authenticity of the Crescent City. But, meeting a person like Mrs. Reed can harken you back to a time and a place and a way of doing things that the rest of the country just doesn't know. The impression she leaves and her personality are larger than life; and her large hats match her multiple outfits.

This photograph on page 46 is from 1996. I happened to have a camera on me when they were descending the stairs to go to the Zulu Ball, the largest African American carnival organization since 1916.

In 2014, my mom met Mrs. Reed in her house. My mom, the former Pan Am flight attendant from the glamour years of the 1950s met Mrs. Reed, the former model. From that one meeting, it was apparent that we had met a woman of consequence. On the flight back to Virginia, my mom told my brother and his wife that we had met a Grand Dame.

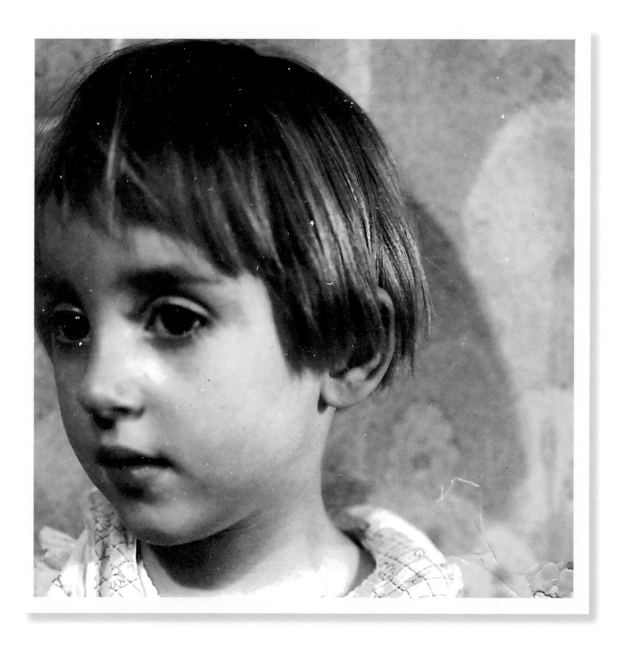

21

"To this place, and the kindness of these people, I owe everything."

— *President Abraham Lincoln, about Springfield, Illinois*

Skinny Ginny and the Old Neighbor Couple

My mom, Virginia, was nicknamed, "Skinny Ginny" as a child since she ran around the yard a lot, and that made her thin, apparently.

In 1935 my mom's family, the Loepps, still lived in Morningside, a part of Sioux City, Iowa. The picture on the opposite page is of my mother at around that time. The picture to the right shows the front porch of the Morningside house with my mom's older brother and sister, Uncle Dave and Aunt Reesy, around 1930. The picture below, to the right is their father (my grandfather), David Loepp.

The next door neighbors were a very old and kind couple, the Larkins. They would sit on their front porch and my grandfather would visit them and ask questions. Three-year-old Skinny Ginny would run up to her dad on their porch. Other times, the elderly Mr. And Mrs. Larkin would sit on the Loepps' front porch and my grandfather would ask them more questions; and my mom, the toddler, would run up to her dad and hear what they were saying. What was so interesting that my mother's father, David F. Loepp, kept asking the old couple, the Larkins, all these questions? It turns out that Mr. and Mrs. Larkin were from Springfield, Illinois and knew Abraham Lincoln and Mary Todd Lincoln before he became the 16th President of the United States. Some of my mom's earliest memories are of hearing these conversations between her dad and this nice older couple about the Springfield lawyer who would later become the only wartime president during a civil war, the Great Emancipator, and so much more.

22

"Experience has taught me how important it is to just keep going, focusing on running fast and relaxed. Eventually pain passes and the flow returns. It's part of racing."

— Frank Shorter

He Was Home in Time for Dinner

Happy 4th of July. In high school, I thought I was the first one of my family to run cross country and track, but then I recalled my dad once barely mentioned that he ran in high school up in Boston; the result of his Spanish teacher (also the cross country coach) telling him that he would get a bad grade if he didn't join the cross country team. On the opposite page, we see my dad, Ernest Hodgkins, running track for Somerville High School on the left with an S on his chest, traversing the wooden, angled home team track. He also ran in college before transferring to the University of Kentucky. Eight years after I ran track and cross country at Fairfax High, my sister did the same.

Anyway, I wasn't the first. My dad wasn't even the first. My great grandfather (my father's father's father) Walter Hodgkins on Thanksgiving Day, 1893, ran into his house in Cambridge, Massachusetts and excitedly told his wife, Maggie (I met Maggie at her 100th birthday party in July of 1975), how he had just won The Cross Country Race while she was making Thanksgiving dinner. He showed her the trophy as proof. As he belonged to the CAA (Cambridge Athletic Association), that makes him one of the top runners in all of Cambridge, perhaps even Boston.

Walter and his brother, George Harry (aka G Harry or just Harry) were two of the top athletes in Cambridge and Boston in the 1890s. They may have also belonged to the BAA (Boston Athletic Association), but I'm not sure yet. The BAA started the Boston Marathon in 1897. In the Hodgkins family, we like to say that Walter won the precursor to the Boston Marathon.

The CAA used to sponsor large track and field games attended by thousands of people and the press throughout the year, including holidays like 4th of July.

After the turn of the century, Walter and Harry were too old to compete, so Harry continued with the CAA for the rest of his life as a judge, announcer, measurer, referee and director of the games. The BAA and perhaps the CAA had supplied athletes to the U.S. Olympic team in 1896 and following years. The photos on pages 54 and 55 show Cambridge newspaper articles describing the Cambridge/Boston games on the 4th of July in 1901 mentioning my great grandfather's brother, Harry as a measurer and in 1904 as the director of the games.

It turns out that Walter and Harry's father (my great great grandfather), who emigrated from England to Boston in 1873, was also a great athlete.

THE FOURTH.

The celebration of the Fourth in this city was a quiet one and "rational" enough for the most critical.

There were no accidents reported by the police. Only four arrests were made for disturbance of the peace by the discharge of firearms, three in division 3 and one in division 2. Those arrested were Manuel Costello, 21; Horatio Allen, 23; John J. McCarthy, 30; and George P. Larrey, 22. There were 13 arrests for drunkenness in division 2 between Saturday and Monday nights and two in division 3.

The amateur athletic events on Cambridge field at 10 o'clock were attended by several hundred persons. The games were run off under the direction of B. B. Osthues and Harry Hodgkins. They included a 100-yard dash, 880-yard run, 440-yard run, one-mile run and a boys' race.

Three heats were necessary in the 100 yards. In the first heat George Goldberg, Boston, the 8½-yard man, came in first, and J. A. Colahan, St. Alphonsus, 6 yards, second. The second heat

My grandfather's brother, Harry Hodgkins, mentioned in a Cambridge newspaper as the Director of Games for the 4th of July games in 1904.

Clerk of course, William Duml
North Cambridge A. C.; assistant:
liam Hynes, C. G. A.; Wiliam Mal
James T. A. S.

Scorer, William Cronan, C. G. /
sistants, Walter E. Colby, Boston
Edgar L. Bean, Boston Herald.

Announcer, Jere. Corkery, Cam
council, Knights of Columbus; ass
Edward L. Murvihill, Cambridge.

Measurers, G. Harry Hodgkins,
Clements, Cambridge.

Inspectors, Joseph B. Brassil, C.
H. H. Harrison, Cambridge Tr
James Cox, Cambridge Times; Jai
Bean, Cambridge Chronicle; Lo
nant, Boston Journal; John B. \
key, Boston Globe; Joseph E. Sl

My grandfather's brother, Harry Hodgkins, mentioned in a Cambridge newspaper as Measurer for the 4th of July games in 1901.

23

"I can never consent to being dictated to as to what I shall or shall not do. I, as President, shall be responsible for my administration. I hope to have your hearty co-operation in carrying out its measures. So long as you see fit to do this, I shall be glad to have you with me. When you think otherwise, your resignations will be accepted."

— Cabinet meeting (1841), as retold by John Alexander Tyler.

The Old Man with his Two Dogs

Meeting the Grandson of the 10th President of the United States: In 2013 I met Harrison Ruffin Tyler, President John Tyler's grandson, at the family's ancestral plantation home below Richmond, VA on the James River, Sherwood Forest. How can this be possible? His father, Lyon Gardiner Tyler, had children in his 70s with a second wife, and that man's father did the same in his 60s with a second wife. This man only drove his SUV over to us to meet a pretty woman, my sister, during our tour. He was not happy with being photographed. He does resemble his grandfather, the president from 1841 to 1844. Check the birth and death dates on the President's and his son's tombstones at Hollywood Cemetery in Richmond on the James.

Tyler was part of the most famous campaign slogan in American history: Tippecanoe and Tyler Too. The first word indicating where the 9th president, William Henry Harrison, had fought Indians in the War of 1812. Harrison had the shortest term (one month) after giving the longest inaugural address (two hours), without a hat or coat. He may have died of pneumonia.

President Tyler started as a Whig, but unhappy with the president's choices, the Whig Party kicked him out. He was an outlaw; a Robin Hood, if you will. He delighted in the moniker, thus, upon buying a new plantation home in 1842, he named it Sherwood Forest.

Called the Traitor President and ranked as one of the worst by pundits, Tyler is the only former president to become a citizen of a foreign (enemy) country, the Confederate States of America. He was voted to their

Congress in 1861, but died in 1862 before being seated. His death was not noted by the United States. He did set up the Washington Peace Conference, to no avail.

Tyler's accomplishments: He set the Maine-Canada border, avoiding war with Great Britain; he told the number one naval power on earth, Great Britain, to leave Hawaii to the United States, and it worked; he gave Texas statehood, gambling that a weak Mexico could be beaten. He opened trade with China, anticipating that the United States would become a Pacific power before even having a West Coast.

As the first Vice President to take over upon the death of a president, he was called The Accidental President and His Accidency. Some people thought there should be a new election. John Quincy Adams called him the Acting President. Opponents sent mail addressed to, "Vice-President-Acting President." Tyler returned those letters unopened. The Secretary of State, Daniel Webster, told Tyler that the Cabinet votes on decisions and majority rules. Tyler rejected that, took the oath and said he was in charge. Thanks to the Tyler Precedent, VPs like Teddy Roosevelt, Truman and LBJ could take over without question.

I saw stacks of the White House China with the official emblem, unused since 1844, hidden away in a cabinet. I saw a Ginkgo Tree, a gift from Commodore Perry who opened up trade with Japan and China, in the backyard since 1855.

Union troops under General Grant occupying Sherwood Forest in 1864 gave their own judgment of the former president by smashing his death mask and attempting to burn the house down. A slave rushed in and put the small fire out. Even today, you can see the burn marks on the wooden floor and damage done to the front door by the Yankees.

John Tyler, a protege of Thomas Jefferson, ruined his reputation by joining the Confederacy; then his son, Lyon Gardiner, spent a lifetime trying to resurrect his father's good name. He argued with Teddy Roosevelt who called Tyler, "monumentally little." One thing Lyon did resurrect was the College of William and Mary, closed for seven years for lack of funds; a result of the Civil War. He became president of that institution for many years. The grandson of President Tyler, who I am standing next to, Harrison Ruffin Tyler, went to William and Mary, like his father, grandfather, Thomas Jefferson and other notables. With his Chemistry degree, he made some sort of invention and created a chemical company, later selling it for over $400 million. With some of that money, he was able to restore his grandfather's beloved Sherwood Forest.

The bust of President John Tyler, the 10th President of the United States, on his gravestone at Hollywood Cemetery in Richmond, Virginia.

24

"Everyone behaves badly--given the chance."

— *Ernest Hemingway, The Sun Also Rises*

"Nobody ever lives their life all the way up except bullfighters."

— *Ernest Hemingway, The Sun Also Rises*

Ernest and Virginia See a Movie on Broadway, October 25, 1957

After serving in the Army for three years in Oahu, Hawaii, my dad, Ernest Hodgkins, was discharged in September of 1957. After three years of sunbathing every possible moment and cracking skulls as a military policeman when needed, he was so ready to move on with his life that he actually threw away all of his uniforms. The ship that brought him also brought his 1940's black sedan to San Francisco where he was going to meet his girlfriend, a Pan Am flight attendant he met at Diamond Head. That flight attendant who flew the Asia routes out of San Francisco was my mother, Virginia Loepp. You can see, on the opposite page, the photo of them on their dinner date in early October, 1957 in the city of hills by the bay.

From there, they flew to New York City so Ernie could be introduced to his future mother-in-law, Matilda Loepp of Sioux City, Iowa. He met her and then went home to his mother in Boston, Massachusetts. Virginia was able to give her mother (my grandmother) a trip around the world for free. She only had to pay the tax, $134. My mom flew with her mother to Europe. Somewhere after Denmark they split up. My grandmother, a devout Catholic, was able to go to the Vatican. She rode a camel in Egypt. She flew from Japan to America to get home. Meanwhile, my mom ended up in Khrushchev's Soviet Union after checking out some Scandinavian and Baltic countries. In Moscow, the Russian tour guides would keep a close eye on the foreign tourists. Only recently did Premier Khrushchev strike a deal with President Eisenhower to allow American tourists in the USSR. So, the tour guides knew they would be in serious trouble if they lost track of an American.

My mom flew back to NYC where my dad drove down from Boston to meet her at the airport and take her to a movie theater on Broadway Avenue. They decided to see *The Sun Also Rises*, a Hemingway story with my mom's favorite movie stars, Errol Flynn, Ava Gardner and Tyrone Power. Someone told my mom that she looked like Ava Gardner. Anyway, my mom really enjoyed the movie even though she knew the three legendary actors were a little too old for the parts they were playing.

This is most likely the conversation they were having as they exited the theater on Broadway in the late afternoon of October 25, 1957. They noticed newspaper boys with a commotion around them. Apparently something really big happened earlier in the day necessitating a rush to reprint and push the new headline out to the streets.

Several hours before Ernie and Virginia went to see *The Sun Also Rises*, at 10:30 AM over on 56th St and 7th Ave, two gunmen wearing Aviator sunglasses, scarves over their faces and fedora hats, burst into the barbershop of the Park Sheraton Hotel and found Albert Anastasia, one of the heads of the Five Families, getting a shave and a haircut in chair #4. One of the men used the muzzle of his gun to push the barber out of the way. After the first spray of bullets, incredibly, Anastasia lunged out of the chair at the gunmen. In his confusion, he actually lunged at their reflections in the barbershop mirror. They sprayed him again and that was the end. Some Mafia used to leave calling cards with a black hand on their victims' bodies. The updated, modern twist with the Anastasia killers was they wore black gloves on their trigger hands.

As a result of Anastasia's confusion with the mirror, the Park Sheraton had the barber chairs turned around so the backs faced the mirrors. Nobody knows why Anastasia's driver did not stay with him like a proper bodyguard for a major mob boss. He, instead, parked the car underground and took a walk outside.

Albert Anastasia was friends with Bugsy Siegel and Lucky Luciano. Siegel created the first big time casino/hotel in Las Vegas with top entertainment; laying the blueprint for what would become the modern Las Vegas we all know. Luciano put the organization in Organized Crime, after Albert and Bugsy bumped off his boss in 1931. He treated crime families like corporations, with meetings and cooperation. Anastasia became the enforcement arm for Luciano, Murder Inc.; suspected of 500 to 1000 deaths. He was called The Mad Hatter and The Lord High Executioner. Charged with murder four times, let go four times, witnesses had a bad habit of getting shot or disappearing.

Most likely, Vito Genovese had Anastasia killed with Rhode Island hitmen, one of whom, Crazy Joe Gallo, said, "You can just call us the Barbershop Quintet."

The aftermath of this high profile hit job was such pressure on the Mob that it was the beginning of the end for the Five Families of New York.

The fall of 1957 was the beginning of the beginning for my family. Virginia and Ernie got married in Boston only months later in early 1958. A year after a shocking surprise October 25, 1957, there was a pleasant surprise for Ernie and Virginia in October 1958, my oldest brother, Terry, was born; the first of five children born to Ernest and Virginia Hodgkins.

My grandmother (on the left), Matilda Loepp, on her around-the-world trip in the fall of 1957, riding a camel in front of the Great Sphinx and the Great Pyramid of Giza.

25

"I must say I find television very educational. The minute somebody turns it on, I go to the library and read a good book."

— Groucho Marx

How Two Deaf Parents Taught Their Children How to Speak

My cousins Bobby and Gary circa 1965, in the Boston area, perhaps Revere. How did my cousins learn a spoken language (English), when their parents, Aunt Patty (my father's sister) and Uncle Bill, used sign language with each other? Babies need someone to speak to them in order to learn how to speak. The solution for Patty and Bill was to put their little boys in front of the TV set.

I never heard positive things about TV growing up, only warnings. My dad used to call it The Idiot Box. My mom would tell us not to sit too close lest we get radiation. Pre-remote control days, we sat close in order to change the channel. Finally, here is a positive tribute to the power of TV.

As their parents were expert lip-readers, Bob and Gary knew how to mouth words without shouting or even using complete sentences as I remember. They understood how to do verbal shortcuts that worked. When Patty and Bill were growing up in Boston, schools for the deaf taught lip-reading and discouraged sign language. The idea was that they will be better acclimated to the wider world where people aren't deaf. That idea was probably a mistake. Of course, now schools for the deaf teach and encourage sign language. But, my siblings and my parents and I successfully talked and conversed with Patty and Bill, with Bill telling jokes and talking about the Celtics.

And what of the experience of talking to the two brothers who picked up spoken language from the TV set? Gary is very funny, especially when telling hilarious stories about himself. I think he speaks some Spanish now, as he married a woman from Colombia. Bob is loquacious, accomplished, and ever so friendly, having mastered many disciplines, academic and otherwise.

26

"The soldier above all others prays for peace, for it is the soldier who must suffer and bear the deepest wounds and scars of war."

— Douglas Macarthur

"Hodgkins, Get Off the Plane": Why My Uncle Refused to Fly in Airplanes

Happy Veterans Day. My father, on the left, joined the Army in 1954. His brother, Ronnie, joined the Navy. Their mother (my grandmother), Muriel, is in the middle. I understand that Ronnie left home at age 16 and joined the Navy and stayed in for 20 or more years. The middle brother, Dick, not in this picture, joined the Marines. Dick was sent to Korea during the Korean War. Despite some stories Dick told, he did not see action, as he was at a desk somewhere. This did not preclude Dick from trauma and a lifetime of effects. According to my uncle, he and his unit were due some R&R in Tokyo. He was sitting with the whole group in this junker military transport plane when someone shouts through the doorway, "Hodgkins" and waves him off the plane. That plane goes on to crash into the side of a mountain in Japan. I can't prove or disprove that story, but my mom confirmed to me that once Dick got back to the U.S., he never flew in a plane again for the rest of his life. He was afraid of all transportation except for cars. In fact, he may have missed seeing his brother, my dad Ernie, alive before Ernie passed away in January of 1995 because he would not fly. So, Dick and his wife drove to Fairfax, Virginia all the way from Boston, and we saw Dick and Ollie at my dad's funeral. Ironically, two weeks later, in order to teach English abroad for one year, I would take two airplanes for 14 hours to the place that apparently affected Dick so profoundly: a wealthy, peaceful, and democratic South Korea.

27

"People have got to know whether or not their President is a crook. Well, I'm not a crook. I've earned everything I've got."

— President Richard Nixon at a November 17, 1973 news conference

Why I Blamed my Sister for Nixon's Resignation

Christmas Day, 1974, Hunter St., Fairfax, VA: The camera caught (opposite page) the very moment I, at age 8, discovered that I got unquestionably the coolest toy of the era, Rock'em Sock'em Robots featuring the Blue Bomber and the Red Rocker where one tries to knock the other's block off and vice versa.

I thought this toy was the most important thing that happened that day, but upon reflection, perhaps my sister, Gina, taking part in this event for the first time was more important. My mom thought so too, as evidenced by the bib she purchased and put on her for that day that reads, "My First Christmas."

Four months earlier, I had turned eight on August 4th. As a kid, I did not watch or care about the news. In my earliest memory of news, two years earlier at age 6, I do remember hearing the local D.C. news that my parents were watching, where they said a security guard at the Watergate Hotel discovered tape on a door jamb so the door wouldn't lock. He took the tape off. He checked the door later and tape was reapplied to keep the door open. He called the police. There was a burglary in progress at The Watergate. They found five men in suits snooping around the Democratic National Committee Headquarters. Back to my birthday, August 4, 1974. Since I didn't pay attention to news, I thought the world was right. Then, suddenly, five days later the president resigns, and soon after, my sister is born. I conflated the two events and sometimes reversed them. Even to this day, I have to remind myself that Gina wasn't born on August 9; that's when Nixon resigned. For years, I used to joke with my sister on her birthday that everything seemed fine, and then around the time she was born, the world turned upside down; the President of the United States quit and flew away in a helicopter. This must have been Gina's fault. I liked Nixon. He looked, sounded, and acted in a unique way. He was essentially bald with a patch of hair trying to be a widow's peak. He had a deep voice and was energetic, even charismatic. Now, because of Gina, apparently, we were left with boring, tired, bald, uninteresting and uncharismatic President Ford. With my reading of history in later years, I realized these events were unrelated. So too, am I glad the Vietnam War and other news from the 1960s isn't attributed to my day and year of birth.

28

"He also knew a great deal about art, letters, philosophy, and general culture; about almost everything, indeed, except the world he was living in."

— G.K. Chesterton, The Man Who Knew Too Much

The Connection They Were Not Aware of:
The Pan Am Flight Attendant and the 1950's Movie Star

On the South America Route with Pan Am, Dateline Brazil, 1956: A flight attendant, my mom, waited for the 75 passengers to board the Douglas DC-7 from the tarmac up the movable stairway. With a wingspan of 117 feet, four large engines running propellers with a diameter between 12 and 15 feet, this was the last major piston engine-powered airplane before the Jet Age; for this was The Golden Age of Air Travel.

A man with his wife entered the plane, and he was far from home. Apparently, director Alfred Hitchcock liked him, as he starred in four of his movies. He was the lead in *The Man Who Knew Too Much* that year, *Rear Window* two years prior, *Vertigo* two years later; *Rope* with Ray Milland was 1948. This was, of course, Jimmy Stewart, and his movie career was in full swing ever since he won an Oscar for *Philadelphia Story* in 1940; with a brief interlude of WWII.

Before takeoff (this particular time in Rio or Sao Paulo) the flight attendants, including my mother, Virginia Loepp, would hand out gum and lifesaver candies. The passengers would use these items to avoid having their ears pop as they quickly reached a higher altitude. Anyway, Virginia offered the gum or lifesavers to Jimmy Stewart, and he gruffly waved them off, shaking his head and saying, "No, no, no." His wife, Gloria McLean, was embarrassed by her husband's rudeness. She accepted the items with a big smile.

It's too bad that they didn't converse a little, for, there was something the star of *The Man Who Knew Too Much* didn't know; and could've found out with a little chitchat. Thirteen years earlier, in August of 1943, Jimmy Stewart trained on B-24 Liberators with the 445th Bombardment Group at Sioux City Army Air Base, an airport built by Virginia Loepp's father as mayor of said city, David Loepp, well before he went off to the European theater of the same war as James Stewart did. Before Major Stewart flew 20 bombing missions over Europe and two years after winning an Academy Award, Jimmy Stewart crash landed a B-24 Liberator bomber at Sioux City Army Air Base. I believe his front landing gear was torn off. My mom, the former Pan Am flight attendant, was very surprised to hear this information when I told her three days ago.

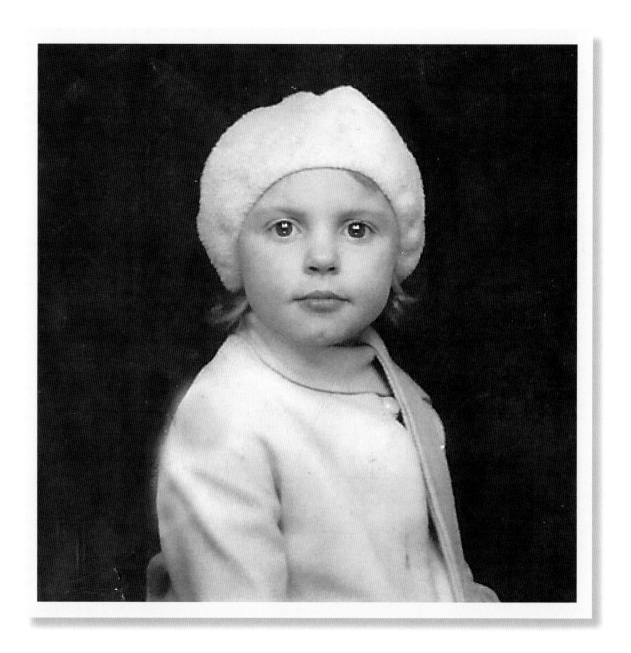

29

"Time is money. Wasted time means wasted money means trouble."

— *Shirley Temple*

A Little Girl with a Plan

Happy 89th Birthday to my Aunt Reesy this weekend past. When Reesy was a small child in Morningside, Iowa (a part of Sioux City, east of the Missouri), her mother (my grandmother, Matilda) would take her hand and walk her one block to the left from the front door and then another left for two blocks. Matilda Loepp with small child in tow would end up at the grocery store and buy all necessary food and items; and perhaps some candy for little Reesy some times. Mrs. Loepp would then take out her checkbook, write a check, and hand it over to the cashier.

One morning in the first half of the Great Depression in the 1930s in Morningside, Iowa, little Reesy got up early before the rest of the household, scribbled some marks on a piece of paper, exited the front door, went one block left, took another left for two blocks, entered the grocery store, picked up some candies, took them to the cashier that her mother had paid so often, handed him the piece of paper she had scribbled on, walked two blocks, took a right, walked one block and returned to her home in Morningside with her newly purchased groceries (candy).

30

"Believe me, every heart has its secret sorrows, which the world knows not, and oftentimes we call a man cold, when he is only sad."

— *Henry Wadsworth Longfellow, Hyperion*

After my Father's Death: Destination Korea

These Pyeong Chang Olympics are fun (chaemi eseyo). My name is Eric. (Che i-reum eun Eric ye yo.) Twenty-three years ago this month, I was called, "Yongeo Sonsaeng nim" (English teacher), in Taejon, South Korea, the 5th largest city located in the middle of the country, a little to the west. Forty-five years after my Uncle Dick (my dad's brother) served in the Korean War as a Marine, five years after I got my English Writing degree from George Mason University, and two weeks after I sat at the front row of my father's funeral, I had arrived in The Land of the Morning Calm after a 14-hour flight from Washington D.C. to Seoul with a stopover in Detroit; with a dedicated group of Korean men smoking in the back of the plane for the full trip.

Picked up by my employer at the airport, at around 4 in morning I was offered a cold drink from a vending machine. In the dark, I thought it was juice or a soda. I took a drink and, to my dismay, it was something called, "iced coffee." That would not be the last time I almost lost my lunch in Korea. I remember thinking this type of drink was a horrible idea that would never catch on. Two years later I would see iced coffee all over Japan.

I was placed in a 4th floor apartment with two Korean-American women. We found that all of our English teacher co-workers also lived on the 4th floors of their apartments too. In fact, I don't think we saw any Koreans on the 4th floors of any of those buildings. Those floors are usually labeled with an F instead of a 4. We found out that 4 sounds like the Chinese word for death, so the Koreans don't want to live on that floor. If you want to find Westerners in Korea, I suggest you go to the 4th floor of any apartment. If I thought, here on the complete opposite side of the globe, I was going to take my mind off the enormity of my father's death, this Sino-Korean superstition was not helping.

The truth is, you can't escape it. I was numb like a zombie walking in a haze for the next year or two.

On my first full day in country, I wandered around this market by myself, not knowing the language, without much or any Korean money and not understanding it anyway. After a while, I noticed in my peripheral view that small people were following me. I turned to look and they hid behind containers. They were children who had not seen any or many Westerners in person. Even though Taejon is a big city, there were very few Westerners there. People would definitely look when I walked by. These children were interested in me, but afraid or shy when I looked toward them. I finally was able to wave them over for this picture. Perhaps this was the answer to my aching soul: the countless cute and curious kids of South Korea that I would come across in classrooms and in the streets like this for the next eight months.

31

"God save thy Grace, King Hal; my royal Hal!"

— FALSTAFF Henry IV, Part 2, Act 5, Scene 5

His Father's Son, Uncle Robby of Sioux City Royalty

Hung be the heavens with black, yield day to night!

Comets, importing change of times and states,

Brandish your crystal tresses in the sky,

And with them scourge the bad revolting stars

That have consented unto Henry's death!

King Henry the Fifth, too famous to live long!

England ne'er lost a king of so much worth.

(Henry VI, Part 1)

My Uncle Robby (my mother's younger brother) passed away a week ago Friday. Robby, like his father, liked to recite Shakespeare. I believe my uncle and his father were autodidacts with a similar intellect. Robby once wanted to discuss with me how F Scott Fitzgerald captured the female voice so well. Robby may have felt the above sentiment for his father as well; the three-term mayor of Sioux City, the man who started college at age 16, the man who left Stanford to go to Chicago Law in order to study under the best law professor in the country, the soldier who was asked by Justice Jackson to sit as judge over the German war criminals at Nuremberg. Yes, Robby and his siblings probably saw their father and mother as royalty, and they were treated as princes and princesses. They got to meet movie stars at the local movie theater who showed up in person for the premieres. They got to go to the iconic New York World's Fair as their father met the iconic Mayor La Guardia. In fact, on May 23, 1939, Mr. And Mrs. Loepp met King George VI and Queen Elizabeth at a dinner reception in Winnipeg, Canada. He was the stammerer featured in the 2010 movie, *The King's Speech.*

If Robby were a Shakespearean character, I think he would be the bard's greatest invention, Falstaff; played by Orson Welles in his favorite invention, *Chimes at Midnight*. Orson, like Robby, lost his father when he was only 15. They both thought their dads were the greatest people they had ever met and mourned them for the rest of their lives. Mr. Loepp was a little strict on his oldest son, David, but lenient with his favorite child, the baby, Robby.

Robby, like Falstaff, a lovable, intelligent, capable wag; he was a popular high school football player who played saxophone, but didn't have time for his age group as he got into jazz clubs underage, dancing the jitterbug, throwing his sister, my mom, in the air over his back. Mrs. Loepp called the clubs looking for her children at least a couple of times.

Falstaff is a comic, lovable character who becomes a tragic three-dimensional person when his best friend and son figure, Prince Hal, becomes King Henry V and turns his back on his old friend in order to grow up and take on the responsibilities of king. Orson Welles turned his back on his own father, a man with many vices. His father died soon after of a broken heart, leaving Orson to mutter for the rest of his life that he killed his own father. In a role reversal or tortured metaphor, Mr. Loepp inadvertently turned away from Robby by simply, tragically passing away in July of 1950. Robby, I believe, would be left with the same feeling as Falstaff being turned away by Prince Hal: abandonment from the friend he loves.

Queen Elizabeth I: I am my father's daughter. (Proving she is as tough and capable as Henry VIII)

All four of Mr. Loepp's children took different paths than he. In later life, would you recognize the Boise, Idaho resident as Sioux City royalty? Yes. He is his father's son; dark German eyes, facial features, deep stage voice, expansive vocabulary, amazing recall, allusions to great literature.

Doesn't time heal all wounds? Did this man actually mourn his father for 67 years? As it turns out, he would talk to some of his seven sons during the day and talk to his father, Marine in WWI and soldier in WWII who passed away in the middle of the 20th century, in his sleep. His sons have heard him speak to his late father: Good to see you sir. I've missed your presence. David, is that you? Are you back from overseas? How's the service treating you?

Uncle Robby will take his rightful place next to his kind, generous mom and his dad who he may have reached out to in his sleep for well over half a century.

Good night, Sweet Prince.

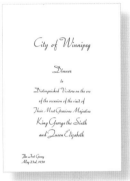

Invitations to Mayor Loepp and Mrs. Loepp for a reception for King George VI and Queen Elizabeth in Winnipeg, Canada, May 23, 1939.

32

"When things don't go well, some coaches might say: run more. Johan Cruyff said: stop for a bit, don't run, analyze and it'll go better."

— *Eusebio*

Scott Hodgkins, the Deadly Quick Winger from Hunter Street

I hope everyone is enjoying the 21st FIFA World Cup. (This would have been the 23rd, but WWII made tournaments for 1942 and 1946 untenable.)

This is a picture of my brother, Scott, playing soccer for Fairfax High School, in the middle, circa 1979. A teacher at the school, Mr. Sabo, volunteered to be the JV (junior varsity) soccer coach. He was a nice man, but he knew he didn't know anything about soccer, so he was smart to hire my oldest brother Terry as the assistant coach. Scott is playing against the team we all hated the most, Annandale. The parents for Annandale club teams would pay professional coaches for their kids. The school would hire expert coaches, not teachers. Their clubs would try to cherry pick the best talent throughout Northern Virginia. When bureaucrats and military moved to the D.C. area with their soccer player sons, they were recommended to move to Annandale. The Fairfax teams from the 1958 (when the players were born) to the 1966 team absolutely hated the Annandale teams. This included the parents. We felt they were cheaters and would do anything to win, and it seemed improper at the time. It also didn't help that they often got first place and would win a lot.

At 5'2" and 110 lbs., Scott was slight of build, but remarkably quick. Just to give you an idea: a 6'0", 185 lb. wide receiver at FHS who held the 100 meter and 4x100 records, spit at Scott in the hallway at school. Astonishingly, Scott spit in this brute's face. This record-holding wide receiver chased Scott up and down every hallway at Fairfax High School in a rage for what seemed like a whole day; and he never caught him.

Back to this particular game. Mr. Sabo had Scott at left fullback. At halftime, Fairfax was losing to the dreaded Annandale 2-0. My brother, Terry, the assistant coach, noticed Annandale had a slow right fullback. Terry whispered to Mr. Sabo to put Scott at left wing in the 2nd half directly facing Annandale's weak link. Terry's analysis was exactly right. Scott tore up their right fullback for a hat trick; Fairfax won 3-2.

In 1990, I sat around the TV with my brothers, Terry, Dave and Scott (soccer players all) watching the 1990 Italy-hosted World Cup with the U.S. participating for the first time since they beat England in the 1950 World Cup hosted by Brazil. We noticed an American player come onto the field. Someone said, "Son of bitch! That is John Stollmeyer from Annandale." As they are both 1962 (age group), Scott played against Stollmeyer much of his life. They actually liked each other and respected each other's abilities and desperate desire to win. In a kind of inside joke, Scott called him "Johnny," and John called him "Scotty" through all those years of soccer, growing up. Scott was actually happy for the Annandale product. Somebody made it to the big time. So, there we were, my brothers and I, cheering for the player from the place that we fought against and hated for most of our soccer lives.

33

"He was the greatest athlete who ever lived.... What he had was natural ability. There wasn't anything he couldn't do. All he had to see is someone doin' something and he tried it ... and he'd do it better."

— 1912 Olympic silver medalist Abel Kiviat about Jim Thorpe

Terry Hodgkins, the Legend of Fairview Subdivision

This is my oldest brother, Terry, eight years older than me, playing stack (center fullback) on Veterans Day of the Bicentennial year battling the hated 1958 (age group/when the players were born) Annandale to a 1-1 tie.

I see he is wearing Patrick cleats made famous by the great 1970s English goal scorer, Kevin Keegan. Also, no shin guards. We would wear our socks down without shin guards because we thought it was cool and we were showing toughness.

He played the three major American sports as a kid and excelled at them. Baseball was a little bit of a problem for him in elementary because although as a pitcher, he had a very powerful throw, he didn't always have control. He would get frustrated and start throwing chin music or beaning the batters. He would lose a lot of ping pong games because he wanted to smash the ball so often. When he had a sleepover at a friend's house, the parents made the mistake of reminding him to tighten the faucet when he is finished in the bathroom. He broke the the thing off. One snow-covered day in the 1970s on Hunter Street, where we lived, Terry threw a snowball so high and far that I lost sight of it, but I know where it landed. Hunter Street ends at Tedrich Boulevard where cars go pretty fast. A car suddenly appeared and the neighbor kids and I saw a snow explosion on the windshield of that car. It careened to a stop. Looking out the window in anger and then disbelief at how far away we were, not wanting to meet the gorilla that could make such a throw, the car continued down Tedrich.

As a sophomore at Fairfax High School, Terry went from 5'8" to 6'3". He could dunk a basketball; and eight years later, Mr. Ward, the hard-nosed football coach and PE teacher wanted to know if I was related to Terry in order to tell me what a great athlete he thought he was. This is very touching coming from the West Virginia man with the buzz cut. There were freaks and jocks. Long-haired smokers were called freaks. Terry had started his smoking habit at age 16. There was one other slang word that later fell into disuse, but described Terry: Frock (freak + jock). In the 1970s, Fairfax High School did not want to inconvenience their student smokers, so they had a smoking lounge for them. Terry says he even sometimes smoked at halftime of his soccer games.

Anyway, in 1976 Terry's Fairfax High School soccer team went to the quarterfinals of State as there were no Regionals back then. He took all the long free kicks and all the throw-ins. His throw-in was used as a corner kick. The other team wouldn't understand why the FHS players were lining up in front of their goal. I had seen his throw-in headed in for a goal. Once I even saw him throw it in to the goalie who didn't expect it and panicked. The ball hit his arm and went in the goal. I have never, at any other time in my life, seen anyone duplicate that.

In 1980, Terry decided to stay with a family in Southampton, England, play on a soccer team, and hope to get noticed by a pro team. We all wished him our best knowing that no American had ever played in the English pro leagues. He was going to Kevin Keegan country, the birthplace of soccer. He quit smoking to prepare himself. Sitting in the Dulles Airport lounge at the beginning of the new decade, Terry watched the jumbo jets take off. As he hadn't flown since he was five, he didn't recall that the wings on jets bend. He was dismayed at just how much the wings on those planes were bending. With thoughts of the wings on his plane breaking off, he found a cigarette machine and promptly resumed his habit. There was a span of several weeks in the summer of 1980 where we thought: maybe, just maybe, Terry made his wildest dream come true.

This is the original photograph taken by a photographer of a local newspaper in the fall of 1976, showing my brother, Terry Hodgkins, heading the ball away as a defender.

Dave Hodgkins (22) and Eike Becker of Fairfax battle Stuart's Luis Pages in playoff soccer. Story, D6.

34

"Fire is the test of gold; adversity, of strong men."

— Martha Graham

Dave Hodgkins, the Constant Competitor Made it to the Bigtime

In this *Washington Post* photograph on the opposite page, number 22 is my brother, Dave (six years older than me), in the playoffs with Fairfax High School against Stuart. The blonde player is Eike Becker, the West German exchange student in 1979. Eike brought his wonderful style of play with him. Such a nice, decent, and affable person, he is still a friend to this day.

In the summer of this year, my brothers, Dave and Scott, would go to England for a soccer tournament. So, my mom called Pete Mehlert, the coach at American University asking if he had any pro contacts in England for Dave. When Pete heard this, he decided to recruit Dave for his team and give him a nearly four-year soccer scholarship.

As a sophomore at FHS, Dave was 5'2", 82 lbs. then he had a growth spurt. His senior year he was 6'2", 175 lbs. The growth spurt enabled him to play in college, but it also had other effects: hip, back and ankle injuries. He was red-shirted his first year at AU, so he wasn't able to join his team against Clemson in the NCAA semifinal where they lost. Clemson won the final. I saw him put on ankle braces that were like a cloth shoe under his cleats that would be tied tight high up the ankle. I also saw tape jobs where he could barely move his feet like he was wearing a cast. With these braces and tape jobs, going into the 1980 season, Dave couldn't do a shooting drill properly. The great but cruel Chinese-American coach, Pete Mehlert, would yell, "You can't shoot, you can't play." One practice, a play called for a pass to the speedster, Scott Snyder (from Scottish Junior National team), but the guy passed it to Dave. Pete yelled, "Don't pass it to Dave. I'm faster than Dave." At halftime of a 0-0 tie with a lowly ranked Loyola team, Pete yelled at his team and within earshot of the opponents, "What we have here is: two bad teams." Pete was one of the top coaches in the country and his players were some of the best: players from the British, Scottish, and Trinidadian Junior National teams; All Met and All-American players from Arlington, McLean, Braddock Road and Fairfax City. Tommy Kramer (Arlington) beat George Mason with seconds left on a free kick from 45 yards out near the half field line. David Nakid (Trinidad) went on to play in the Danish pro league.

Dave Hodgkins would not let injuries stop him. He was an unendingly competitive person. Once the large, powerful, and fast oldest brother, Terry (eight years older than me), threw a dart at Dave that hit him or came close. At the time, the small, skinny, and fast Dave, picked up Terry from behind and body-slammed him on the basement floor at Hunter Street. Dave sprinted up the stairs, out the house, down Carolyn Avenue, sharp left back up Tedrich Boulevard and a left back up Hunter Street with Terry breathing down his neck. Dave used zigzagging and circling around parked cars as a technique. They ran a second lap for about two miles when Mrs. McDermot on Hunter Street saved Dave by getting his attention and opening her front door to him.

The first time I beat Dave in ping pong was in the basement of the Saint Andrews Drive house. My side was near the five wooden steps and door to get out of the basement. The second I won, I turned to sprint up the steps, go up through the split-level house to proclaim to our family in the kitchen that I was the king of ping pong. Dave wasn't going to let me out until he beat me. So, he sprinted around the table, dove and tackled me on the steps. Like a horror movie victim, I lunged at the door, missed the door handle and clawed the door to the bottom, as Dave corralled my legs and dragged me down the wooden steps to the hard tile floor. He beat me next game.

Dave's various injuries finally improved. In fact, he became the second leading scorer in 1982 with nine goals in a 12-game season. Pete came around to respect and appreciate Dave. He actually built the offense around Dave, nicknamed, "Hodge." The two official plays that American University had were called, "Hodge 1" and "Hodge 2."

The taker of the free kick would raise his hand and shout, "Hodge 1" and he would kick it to Dave's head. The newly healthy Dave would hold off the defender and get up in the air and flick the ball backwards with his head. When the kick is taken, two speedsters would take off, being level with Dave when the ball reaches his head, then crisscross behind him as he heads it to one of the two. That person should then have the ball land at his feet, and should then have a one-on-one with the goalie.

The year that AU basketball beat Patrick Ewing's Georgetown Hoyas, Dave won Senior Athlete of the Year. A year after Dave graduated, American University played UCLA in the NCAA championship and lost in eight overtimes, 1-0. He was happy for his old teammates.

In his house, I have stumbled across physical therapy devices, bands, balls and other injury-fighting tools, as Dave talks about the various sports he's preparing to play; including ping pong.

HEADS-UP: AU striker David Hodgkins set up Tom Kramer's game-winning goal against Hofstra in the ECC title game Saturday. The Eagles won 1-0. Story, page 13. Photo by Ronald W. Thomas.

A picture of my brother, Dave Hodgkins, from the front page of the American University newspaper, The Eagle, showing him assisting a game-winning goal with his head.

35

"Life is about timing and overcoming difficult things."

— Carl Lewis

Hayes Woods, the Lightning Bolt from School Street

Happy belated Fourth of July. Hayes Woods had surgery on the vertebrae in his neck. He has had several back surgeries since an accident at a gas company job in 2000. Holding a rope connected to a huge measuring device, the rope gave way and ruptured multiple discs. This was at least a two-man job. The other guy was sick.

While visiting Hayes at the hospital, he invited me to his sister's 4th of July party out in Manassas. I was completely surprised to see Mr. Tom Payne (on my left) at the Woods' cookout. I remember in 1984 my family went to a large School Street (traditional black neighborhood of Fairfax City) cookout. The Woods and the Paynes used to live there until developers bought up the land in the 1990s, dispersing the original neighbors around Virginia and out of state as far away as Florida.

My mom asked me to find out how Mrs. Payne (Nettie) was. Hayes already told me in the hospital that she had passed away three years ago. So, with a heavy heart, in July of 2018, I showed Mr. Payne the photo on page 95 from 1975, showing his wife, Nettie, talking to my mom with my little sister, Gina, in tow with our pet dog, Oliver. Oliver never had a leash and never needed one. I knew that Mr. Payne had lost his son, Roger, in 1983. To be honest, I got choked up talking to the man who had lost his wife and one son.

My mom and Nettie would talk and laugh the whole game. I was always curious about what was so funny. It was clear that Mr. And Mrs. Payne were very enjoyable to be around. She was the biggest person with the biggest laugh on the sidelines, while Tom was the skinniest with a reserved smile. We could spot them right away when we pulled up in the Eleven Oaks school parking lot near the School Street neighborhood and its Baptist Church on Chain Bridge Road.

Nine years before the picture of my mom and Nettie Payne, Eleven Oaks was in its last year as an all-black school. Twelve years after Brown vs Board of Education (1954) prescribed desegregation the law of the land, there were still two all-black schools in Northern Virginia; Eleven Oaks was one of them. Southern governors were obstructionists for much of this time, then finally in 1966, the process was complete when the students from Eleven Oaks started going to Green Acres.

Hayes is five years older than me, so he played soccer with my brothers, Scott and Dave. He remembers his first year of school at Eleven Oaks: all his classmates were black. Then, he remembers that he suddenly had white classmates in his second year of school, this time at Green Acres. The funny thing is that the year before, the after-school and summer programs were already desegregated. I had noticed in the 1970s that something was unusual about James Payne's (Tom and Nettie's oldest son) eye. It turns out he is blind in one eye due to a childhood accident. Hayes says that at the newly desegregated Green Acres, James was pulling little Hayes in a wagon, looked back at Hayes, faced forward and ran into a part of a fence, injuring James.

In Hayes' first soccer game ever as a little kid, he scored four goals due to his tremendous speed. Hayes didn't know all of the rules of this brand new sport, so when he saw the opposing goalie hold the ball, Hayes tackled him American football style, took the ball and kicked it in. When the referee kicked him out of the game, little Hayes cried. Hayes was probably the fastest person at Fairfax High School that no one ever timed. He and Alan Cohen vied for right wing on the FHS soccer team. Alan could beat him in 50 yards, and Hayes could beat everyone in 100 yards. He raced a large football player named Louie Simmons, a legendary muscleman and athlete who went on to play on scholarship in college, in the high school field house. I believe this race would be between 50 and 100 yards. Louie liked to run barefoot. Anyway, he was very surprised Hayes tied him. As an adult, Hayes was on the same soccer teams as my brothers and me. He always blew by people. Hayes says that when he blew out his knee, he had the same doctor as Carl Lewis, the Olympic gold medalist. Hayes says he challenged Carl Lewis to a race when they recovered. I think Carl laughed when he turned him down. Hayes Woods from School Street did not laugh.

My mother, Virginia Hodgkins, with Nettie Payne, my sister, Gina, and our dog, Oliver, watching a soccer game at Eleven Oaks Elementary School soccer field, 1975.

36

*"No matter what activity or practice we are pursuing, there isn't anything that isn't made easier through constant familiarity and training.
(I think you can apply this to soccer as well.)"*

— Dalai Lama

Eric Hodgkins, the Single-minded Pursuit from Age 7 to Age 19 (1974-1985)

My mother says I practiced soccer eight hours a day as a kid. I basically didn't play with toys from age 7 on. I would grab a used soccer ball and run outside. We made little goals on Hunter Street in front of our house with shoes or clothes. I was only goalie at first because I was too young and in the way for my brothers and their friends (4, 6, and 8 years older than me). When they weren't around, I would practice by myself. I was finally able to be a viable player with the older kids around age 9. The breakthrough came from juggling the ball over 100 times using my feet, thighs, head, and in 5th grade my shoulders. I could balance the ball on my head, catch it with either foot, catch it with my neck and flick it back in the air. The Van Kamps' yard had a crabapple tree with two branches forming a V. I would practice chipping with both feet from the Wisemans' yard through the V. I would practice give-and-goes passing it off the Muncie's tires in a dramatic game time way with choreographed moves before and after the pass. At school, I would crumple up a piece of paper and juggle it with my feet. Coming home from Layton Hall Elementary, I would dribble a piece of gravel with give-and-goes against the curb for half a mile before shooting the gravel into a sewer opening.

Over the past several World Cups, we have seen these various tricks in commercials, so I will tell you five things I could do that I have not seen anyone on TV or in person do: at night on Saint Andrews Drive, I would kick the ball 25 feet straight up in the air to gently touch the street light, come back down, not letting the ball touch the ground and do it again with the left foot. With head and feet, I would juggle the ball 10 to 20 feet in the air. I could kick a corner kick and hit the side post on purpose. Lastly, I could juggle the ball on my feet while running forward fairly fast.

All was right with the world. I was starting center half and my brother, Terry, was our coach. He was the best coach I had seen. On every soccer field, I felt I was the most skilled player there because of the teachings from Terry over the years.

Suddenly, a small cabal of parents committed a coup and ousted my teenage/young adult brother. Maybe they thought they could get a fancy coach with college connections.

The team disbanded, so I had to try out for another Fairfax (FPYC) team with a bunch of strangers who didn't respect me and a coach who relied on metrics; he liked using a stopwatch all the time. These kids were big, fast, and strong. I was tall, skinny, and slow. The coach would give spreadsheets to the parents showing how fast or athletic the players were. I barely made this team. The coach made me a substitute for the first time in my life, and took away much of my playing time. Also, he put me in as center forward, a position I never played or liked, as I am a natural half back. I like to assist, not score. You need speed and strength to be a goal scorer. He was setting me up to fail; or so he thought. What these people didn't know was tall, skinny, slow Eric had played against people much faster and more athletic than them his whole life on Hunter Street, Saint Andrews Drive, and at Van Dyke Park; against his brothers and their teammates/friends (4, 6, and 8 years older than Eric).

In a 10-game season, off of the bench, I led the team in scoring with eight goals; scoring with both feet and head balls too. Remember, because of Terry coaching me, my technique was better than these strong, fast guys.

I scored in two ways that I have not seen repeated by anyone. I kicked a corner kick into the goal on purpose, using the inside of my right foot to curve it in. Terry used to call that a "banana ball." In another game, I was tired with a quick defender on me. The goalie was a little shaky and the sun was in his eyes, so pinned to the sideline about 40 yards away, I decided to bounce the ball in front of me, with my left shoulder shielding the defender away, with all of my strength, I launched a right footer straight up with a huge ark toward the goal. The ball came down to within an inch of the crossbar, and with a mis-timed jump, the ball hit the keeper's arms and head, and went in.

In practices during shooting drills, I always made sure to murder the ball with either foot always on goal; often aimed at the goalie. The goalie would duck so he didn't get his head taken off. In taking this power shot, I would jump in the air for power and to keep the ball down. Also, I would go after the coach's son every chance I got. He was a very good fullback; big and strong. In a corner kick drill (7 on 7), I scored 6 goals in a row, two off of him. He backed down and asked somebody else to cover me. His dad, the coach, ended the drill early. This kid played fullback for South Carolina University.

Annandale hired a professional coach, Mr. Dugan, who asked me to try out for his team. He only gave me five minutes of playing time and apologized. College coaches would later recruit from his team.

I later faced this new superstar Annandale team with the future college players (I saw at least one on George Mason later.). The coach's son scored for us. Annandale responded with the equalizer. I was subbed in late as a center forward against the new-look skilled, athletic Annandale Red Rockets. I would not leave fullbacks alone. I would run at them knowing they did not have elite control and would get nervous with me making a straight full speed run at them while they are trying to control a bouncing ball. I took the ball from him and while it was still bouncing high, I took a full volley with my left foot from the left side of the 18-yard line to the upper right-hand corner, pegging the bottom of the crossbar, hitting the keeper in the arm and going in. I later watched many of these people play college ball.

IN TROUBLE is the Annandale Red Wings' Warren Getler as the Fairfax Police Youth Club's Roger Payne (left) and Keith Hix close in on him, Trailing the action is Mickey McDermott of Fairfax.

37

"Pele doesn't die. Pele will never die. Pele is going to go on forever."

— Pele

Roger Payne, My Childhood Hero of the 1970s

The blonde kid in the picture on page 103 is me leaning against Roger Payne's knee, circa 1974. The photo on the opposite page is from a local newspaper in June, 1973 showing my brother, Scott's teammate, Roger going after an Annandale Red Wing. I see he is wearing knee pads like football players used to wear. Scott says he wore those because he was expecting to rumble through the other team; he was ready to do battle. Big, explosive, fast (probably the fastest and most powerful in the league), Roger would score one to two goals a game. He was the star of the team. When Roger was chasing down a long-ball behind the opposing defense, the parents and spectators would inch toward the sideline and lean forward knowing he may score. Like no other player, he would rocket the ball into the goal, snapping the net. At the Eleven Oaks School soccer field near his School Street neighborhood, Roger would also rocket the ball over the goal way off into the woods; and the poor goalie had to find it while we waited. Coincidentally, my family and I saw, in the same month and year as this newspaper photo, the greatest soccer player who ever lived with his Santos club team from Brazil defeat the Baltimore Bays at Memorial Stadium 4-0. Pele put on a show at the end with a quick goal. In my six-year-old's mind, I saw Roger as a Pele.

In addition to being teammates and forwards with Roger, my brother, Scott, was good friends with him. Often, the only white kid, Scott was invited to Roger's birthday parties; always at Regional Parks like Bull Run Regional Park.

Roger's older brother, James, a very nice and humble person who suffered a permanent eye injury in childhood, went to all of his younger brother's games. James wouldn't talk about himself. He would change the conversation to proudly talk about his brother, Roger. It seems that James looked up to his younger brother.

On an otherwise unremarkable day in 1983, Roger Payne did not survive a car accident. As he was in the Army, I was told he was driving from base in Tennessee, trying to make it back to School Street in Fairfax City.

Now 16 years old at the Baptist Church at the top of School Street, waiting in line at Roger's wake to greet his mother, Nettie, I was speechless. She recognized me and continually crying, hugged me. I did not properly mourn Roger, as I was worried Nettie wouldn't recognize me and that I wouldn't know what to say. I said nothing.

Thirty-three years later, at work I showed my coworker an old soccer team photo with Roger and my brother in it; shared to me through an app on my phone. Recognizing Roger in this photo, I excitedly told my coworker about Roger. For the first time in over three decades, I was talking about Roger; and effusively. But, then my voice cracked. I got choked up. I couldn't finish talking about Roger.

I am taken aback by this discovery about myself: I can't talk about Roger Payne without getting choked up. In the last year or so, I have tried to talk about Roger to several other people only to be unable to finish. I am truly surprised. I will admit that I have cried over the loss of Roger Payne 35 years ago. I think I have finally properly mourned my friend.

If I could talk to Roger's mother, Nettie, about her son, I would say that when I was 4, 5, 6, 7 and 8, Roger, a big superstar kid I thought of as Pele, befriended a shy, mumbling, blonde kid who would look down while talking. With tubes in my ears, I couldn't hear so well either. He not only noticed me but took delight in hanging out with me. We were buddies. I could not believe my luck. I think I was the younger brother he didn't have. He was my own personal Pele; my childhood hero permanently stuck in the era from 1970 to 1975.

When I discovered this slide last year in a group of 700, looking through a slide viewer, I reacted with a shout. I never knew my father took this photo, but I immediately knew who it was. The memories came back instantly. My dad, who passed away in 1995, knew this image was special; that's why he snapped it.

Sudden memories of Roger: at Eleven Oaks School, Roger jumped on a bike, did a wheelie for 50 yards, up and down a hill, never letting the front wheel touch the ground. I was in awe.

Right after a game, when I was 5 or 6, the superstar, Roger, pointed me out with a big laugh and warm smile, said in a friendly way, "I remember you when you were just a snot-nosed little kid." He was delighted to see me, to my surprise. This was a cute compliment to me. He was suggesting that I wasn't a little kid anymore, even though I was.

When the final whistle blew, I would lean looking for my new friend, and the star, Roger, would weave around parents and other big people to find his new friend, me.

Me hanging out with my pal, Roger Payne, watching a soccer game at the Eleven Oaks Elementary School soccer field, circa 1974.

38

"…Over there, over there
Send the word, send the word over there
That the Yanks are coming
The Yanks are coming…"

— Song, Over There by George M. Cohan, 1917

100-Year-Old Effects and Thoughts from my Grandfather

The 11th hour of the 11th day of the 11th month is the centennial of the armistice ending The Great War, The War to End All Wars, The War for Democracy, The War of Nations, The European War, and finally World War I (for tragic future reasons).

My grandfather (my mother's father), David Loepp, was a Marine in WWI and is somewhere in this group photo (opposite page) in France. The pictures on page 107 show the front and back of a postcard with David on the front. We can see that this is a French postcard from the printed French words on it. These types of postcards appear to be a nice service for foreign allied soldiers. You can see that he was in Bordeaux and that he sent this 55 days after the Armistice. I think David sent this back to his German-speaking mother either at a farm in Iowa or South Dakota.

Turning back to the group photo, notice there are several different nationalities with several different military uniforms here. The French female nurses are wearing all white including the headwear. There are several wounded soldiers. You can see eyepatches, head bandages and crutches. The hats indicate different ranks and that they are soldiers of different nations. There is one African soldier. One man is wearing a Russian style hat. There are clearly French, British and American troops here. Before you try to figure this 100-year-old photograph out, I should tell you what my grandfather wrote in a letter about this picture to his mother: the soldiers thought it would be funny to swap hats before the photo was taken. Americans and Brits are wearing French hats, Frenchmen are wearing American hats and so on.

The Great War had ended before my grandfather could be sent to the Western Front. He stayed in France many months more and took French and Law courses; and perhaps others at the Sorbonne in Paris. I have read grandfather David Loepp's letters written before, during and after the Armistice, where he gives his impressions of President Wilson, the Kaiser, the Armistice, the Treaty of Versailles (before it commenced); he inspected battlefields post war and unchanged. In the end, it seems that he simply wanted to get back home to America, carry on with personal and family duties; and see his brothers and mother.

LES FÊTES DE LA VICTOIRE A PARIS — 14 JUILLET 1919
Avant le Défilé - Les Maréchaux PÉTAIN & FOCH

A postcard brought home by Private Loepp showing two of the top war heroes of France in World War I, Marshal Petain and Marshal Foch.

A postcard that Private David Loepp sent home to his mother from France with his picture on the front.

Yours truly,
Pvt D. F. Loepp
Bordeaux, France
January 5, 1919

CARTE POSTALE

M